A SEARCH FOR
PURPLE
COWS

A SEARCH FOR PURPLE COWS

A TRUE STORY OF HOPE

SUSAN CALL

Guideposts

New York

A Search for Purple Cows

ISBN-10: 0-8249-3441-5
ISBN-13: 978-0-8249-3441-5

Published by Guideposts
16 East 34th Street
New York, New York 10016
Guideposts.org

Distributed by Ideals Publications, a Guideposts company
2630 Elm Hill Pike, Suite 100
Nashville, Tennessee 37214

Guideposts and Ideals are registered trademarks of Guideposts.

Acknowledgments
Every attempt has been made to credit the sources of copyrighted material used in this book. If any such acknowledgment has been inadvertently omitted or miscredited, receipt of such information would be appreciated.

Scripture quotations are taken from The Holy Bible, New International Version. Copyright © 1973, 1978, 1984, 2011 by Biblica, Inc. Used by permission of Zondervan. All rights reserved worldwide. www.zondervan.com

Library of Congress Cataloging-in-Publication Data

Call, Susan.
  A search for purple cows : a true story of hope / Susan Call.
    pages cm
  Includes bibliographical references and index.
  ISBN 978-0-8249-3441-5 (alk. paper)
1. Call, Susan. 2. Christian converts—United States—Biography. 3. Abused women—Religious life. 4. Women—Violence against—United States. I. Title.
  BV4935.C255A3 2013
  277.3'083092–dc23
  [B]

2013018256

Cover and interior design by Müllerhaus
Cover photograph by Shutterstock
Typeset by Aptara, Inc.

Printed and bound in the United States of America
10 9 8 7 6 5 4 3 2 1

CONTENTS

ACKNOWLEDGMENTS

*To my wonderful children, Jennifer and Ryan:
you have been two of the biggest blessings in my life. I wish you
nothing but God's best in your lives. May you always remember
to trust God, because He is forever faithful.*

*Mom and Dad, thank you for being who you are.
You are my heroes in life. Thank you for
blessing me with such an amazing family.*

*Thank you to Christian radio for being the persistent
voice that brought light into my darkness while pointing
me to the true Light; I am eternally grateful.*

THE JOURNEY BEGINS

The elevator *ding* that Monday morning broke through my thoughts as I struggled to gain control of my racing mind. The momentary pause before the door opened when it arrived at the fourth floor of my office building felt like an eternity. I stared at the floor, weary and dejected. I was consumed by brokenness. *How has my life spun so out of control?* I wondered. My world had shattered into a million tiny pieces in the short time since I'd welcomed the start of the weekend Friday afternoon until that Monday morning.

My thoughts and focus were far from the workday ahead. *Can't I just remain here, alone in the elevator?* I thought. *Or maybe I can slip into my office unnoticed. Maybe everyone will leave me alone today.* I exhaled slowly and painted what I hoped was a convincing smile across my face. I planned to hide behind the façade that I was okay, that my world was intact, and that today was just another Monday. Maybe my shallow smile would be enough to hide the overwhelming depth of my pain.

The elevator doors slid open. *I can do this*, I thought, stepping out of the safety of the elevator.

"Good morning," a cheery coworker said as she passed. "Did you have a good weekend?"

I forced my smile to grow. "*Mm-hmm*," I replied with a nod. "Can't believe it's Monday already." I got out of the elevator and started in the opposite direction. "Have a great day," I said, before turning down the hall and slipping into my cubicle.

Did you have a good weekend? played over and over in my mind. *If she only knew*, I thought.

I slid into the chair at my desk, focusing on the blinking cursor that flashed impatiently on my computer screen. I entered my password, grateful to shift my attention to something other than the despair of my crumbling life.

The truth of my private hell would remain a secret as long as I could hide behind the pretense of my happy, perfect life. My coworkers, friends, and family would be none the wiser. I'd let them continue to think I'd managed to acquire the elusive American Dream.

And why would they think otherwise? By all appearances, my husband Joe was a doting husband and father. We lived in a quaint, three-bedroom, split-level home in a sought-after suburb. We had two beautiful children—five-year-old Jennifer and four-year-old Ryan—a golden retriever, Alley, a fenced yard, and even an au pair. Just a few years earlier, I had joined the ranks of the minivan-driving, suburban working moms. My job at a global technology company afforded me the opportunity to pursue professional growth and regularly rewarded my hard work and tenacity with promotional opportunities. Joe too had been recognized as a leader within his organization. Armed with his strong technical aptitude, he welcomed the complex challenges that unfolded daily as a part of his work. You could say that career success had come our way. We were both pleased with the rate at which we were navigating our respective corporate ladders. No, life hadn't been completely perfect, but despite the few rough spots, I remained hopeful. Knowing that everyone deals with some challenges in life, I believed—perhaps even naively hoped—that if I worked harder, tried harder, and perhaps dug just a little deeper, my life would eventually come closer and closer to matching the façade that the world saw daily.

I had met Joe eleven years earlier when I graduated from college and moved from my small hometown in Pennsylvania to Maryland to pursue a job opportunity. It was truly an exciting time of life. Although our paths crossed at my job soon after my move, to be honest, I didn't pay much attention to Joe. Sure, I couldn't help but notice how some of the women in our office tripped over each other hoping to gain Joe's interest. His incredible confidence and dapper style seemed to captivate them. But during that time, I was busy settling into my new life, adjusting to my new job, and making new friends, as well as connecting with others who lived nearby.

One such friend was Blake. We had met a few years earlier, working as counselors at a summer camp outside Philadelphia. Although he was cute, with his blond locks and sun-kissed skin, it was obvious his beauty came from within. The camp, which catered to inner-city youth away from the tough streets for the first time, required a different type of counselor to be truly successful. Blake made it look easy. The kids arrived wide-eyed, untrusting, and unsure. Blake's gentle, kind ways let the children and the other counselors know he was genuine and truly trustworthy. Whether he was taking kids on hikes in the woods to explore the great unknown or sitting up with the other counselors after lights-out, he embraced life and invested in those around him.

Reconnecting with Blake after the years since camp was refreshing. Like me, he had moved to Maryland following college graduation to pursue the job opportunities that abounded in Washington, DC's, thriving suburbs. His move, two years ahead of mine, made him a welcome resource as I explored my new surroundings. I was glad to learn that time had not changed Blake's sincere ways and quickly discovered that he liked many of the same things I did.

I was swept away by my friendship with Blake and was enjoying life. Whether dancing at a club, skiing, taking in a football game, playing backgammon, or just cooking dinner at his apartment, it seemed Blake and I always had fun. He loved going to the beach, and we sometimes drove two hours just to spend a day in the sand and sun or watch the fireworks on the Fourth of July. Sitting on a beach blanket, listening to the rolling crash of waves, and watching the brilliant display across the sky was magical. I found the times I spent with Blake to be the best of times. He made me happy, genuinely happy.

I knew from summer at camp that he was compassionate, but the more time I spent with Blake, the more I realized his heart was big and his family close. Though they lived four hours away, if they needed something, he made it happen. One of the many instances I will never forget happened when Blake's mom went through a tough time. Through illness and physical challenges, she had lost many of her teeth, which was physically difficult but was even more emotionally painful. Blake, knowing how hard this was on her, saved up money to provide her with permanent implants. He even drove the eight-hour round-trip to be with her when she needed his encouragement most.

Over time, I felt as though things were starting to develop between us. Although we never talked about our relationship, I noticed subtle changes between us that gave me hope. Once in a while, Blake would slip his hand into mine, making my heart flutter like a schoolgirl in a romantic movie. I began to hope we could take our friendship to the next level. I wondered if he could possibly have the same feelings for me, though I always dismissed these thoughts, not believing I could ever be good enough for him. Despite my growing interest in Blake, we never talked about our feelings for each other. And even though Blake would occasionally hold my hand, he didn't offer me compliments or say any of those sweet words that so often accompany a budding relationship. I began to dissect our time together and caught myself replaying conversations and analyzing movements. I fell into the awkward trap of analyzing everything—trained by the most popular magazines prominently displayed at grocery-store checkout lines. Taunting titles, such as "10 Easy Ways to Tell if He Likes You," delivered empty promises for determining relationship clarity. I wished I could tell Blake how my feelings had grown for him, but I feared losing my best friend.

As I struggled to make sense of my feelings, a distraction showed up in the form of a good-looking, sharply dressed analyst working in the department next to mine. It was the first time I'd really noticed Joe. Although I had met him not long after I began my job, he had simply been a face in a neighboring department. I've always been horrible with names, so it was no surprise he knew my name long before I knew his. Perhaps that added to the initial mystery and intrigue. Everyone at the office knew Joe, in part because he was so polished. No one was ever surprised when they heard he had been a model during his college years; he was tall, dark, and handsome. Sporting only the best labels and expensive suits, he was always dapper and suave. People noticed when Joe entered a room. His polish was more than just his appearance. Joe brought something different, something more to the table. With a keen business sense and intellect, Joe grabbed people's attention. When he spoke, they listened. Almost mysteriously, he captivated any audience.

Some time after I was introduced to Joe, he began pursuing me. Initially, he was subtle, coy, and flirtatious. I noticed the occasional attention, but I didn't give it a second thought. Instead, I was focused on my new home and my friendship with Blake. Unbeknownst to me, Joe had quickly learned my work routines. A simple trip to the soda machine typically resulted in a chance hallway encounter with Joe. *Coincidence*, I'd thought, though I later learned he had carefully orchestrated those encounters. He used each opportunity to make his interest known; the compliments flowed. "Wow, Susan, you look gorgeous today," he'd say. Or, "Did you have your hair done? It looks fantastic."

I'll admit I was flattered by the attention, but I wasn't interested in Joe. I was hoping for a relationship with Blake. He was the one who had captured my heart and my attention. *If only he would notice me—really notice me*, I thought.

Instead, it was Joe who noticed. In fact, rarely a day went by without kind words from him. He noticed new haircuts, new outfits, everything. Without a doubt, one of the first things that attracted me to him was quite simply that he noticed. What a welcome change it was, not to just have someone notice, but to constantly be showered with compliments. Joe was a charmer, always ready with wonderful affirming words. The scene became part of the fabric of my workday.

"Hi, Susan, how are you today?" Joe would say with a big smile.

"I'm doing well. Busy day in our department, we have a lot of problems to solve today."

"You'd never know you've had a stressful day by looking at you. You look gorgeous."

"Thanks, Joe," I'd say shyly with a smile.

"Keep dressing that sharply. With that and your hard work, it will just be a matter of time until you're the CEO."

Flattered, I'd respond, "Thanks, Joe. I'd better get back to it."

"I'm serious, you know. You're going places, definitely going places. Just remember that you heard it from me first."

But how could I forget? Joe reminded me of his confidence in my bright future often. New to the working world, I welcomed the optimistic support and hopeful thoughts for future career success. Even more, I enjoyed seeing my self-worth from his perspective. After all, what girl doesn't enjoy being told she is beautiful, that an outfit makes her look like a million dollars, or that she is capable of great career success? Joe truly spoiled me with his words.

Soon my heart was torn. I knew I loved Blake, but feeling insecure, I lost confidence that what we had would ever really be more than a friendship. It wasn't enough that Blake spent time with me, made me laugh, took me dancing, or cooked dinner for me. At the young age of twenty-three, I lacked the wisdom to understand our relationship without a tangible definition, a known status, or clear context. What exactly did we have? I didn't want to guess. I didn't want to interpret. I wanted Blake to tell me, clearly tell me, that he wanted to be more than just friends. I dreamed of my own romantic movie moment, one where our eyes would meet, he would pull me close and profess his growing love for me. Realizing that this was probably less than realistic, I knew I would be happy with something far less dramatic, if he could only admit that he was starting to fall for me. I waited longingly for his words to provide clarity—words that were never spoken. As I evaluated our relationship, the one thing I failed to do was consider all of the ways he was showing me he cared for me. Although his actions perhaps should have spoken loudly to me, they fell on my deaf and insecure heart. I feared rejection. I feared losing my best friend. Ultimately, I feared being alone.

My confusion seemed to be magnified when I moved into a new apartment closer to work. I traded an hour-long daily commute for a fifteen-minute drive.

When I found my new place, Blake was excited to visit and see my new home. "Nice place," he said as he stepped into my modest one-bedroom apartment. From the living room you could see into the very small galley kitchen through the large pass-through window.

"I know it's not spacious, but I can afford it," I proudly said as I showed Blake around.

He pulled back the curtains, revealing the sliding door that led to the very small balcony. "Great view," he joked as we took in the less-than-scenic view of a large parking lot and a path to the next building.

"I know!" I laughed. "You're jealous aren't you?"

"It's a cute place, but we'll never see each other," Blake said, his voice quiet.

"Of course we will," I said. "That won't change. But now I just won't have to spend so much time commuting to work."

While my new apartment shortened my travel time for work, it traded the short distance to Blake's apartment for a longer drive. I hoped it wouldn't matter. Tired of the daily stress of heavy beltway rush-hour driving, I didn't think the distance would be as challenging on weekends, which was when I typically saw Blake anyway.

At work, the frequent hallway encounters with Joe progressed into invitations to go out for drinks or dinner. But as much as I loved the compliments and attention, I still wasn't interested in dating Joe. Regardless, he asked me out at least once a week. Later I learned that with each no I gave Joe, his resolve deepened. He pursued me at work; he called and pursued me at home. Week after week, there wasn't a day without multiple conversations with Joe.

Then, with little warning, he stopped giving me any of his attention. I stopped passing Joe in the hallways at work. Trips to the break room no longer included a chance encounter with the debonair analyst from the department next door. His phone calls abruptly stopped. I never did find out why.

It was then that I started to realize how the daily and generous compliments from Joe had become a lifeline to my self-esteem. The flow of compliments filled a void within me that I hadn't even realized was there. When Joe stopped pursuing me, his silence was deafening. I noticed.

I struggled to make sense of my emotions. Confused about my situation with Joe, I still longed for Blake's affection yet doubted he would ever reciprocate my feelings. And Blake had been right. The traveling distance from my new apartment made it much harder for us to get together. Longer stretches of time passed between the times we spent together. My insecurities multiplied.

I missed Joe's constant attention. During the occasional lulls at work I found my mind immediately wandering to thoughts of Joe. *Where is he? What has changed?* I wondered. My heart ached. After so much time with Blake and the consistent compliments from Joe, this suddenly quieter life came as a shock. I feared I had lost the chance for either relationship to work out. I was left with no answers, only confusion.

This new normal lasted a few weeks. Then, on a Saturday that started out as so many others had before it, my pager went off, calling me into the office. In my department, every few days our pager shifted to the next person on call. Together, our team shared the responsibility of providing 24–7 computer support to military hospitals. Escalations or critical software issues required our immediate attention. On what would become a fateful Saturday, a client's system problems trumped my weekend plans. I headed to the office, hoping I could quickly resolve the situation and get back to enjoying my weekend.

I worked swiftly over the next few hours, finally fixing the problem. *Glad that's finished*, I thought as I began entering my notes into our tracking system. Suddenly I heard the sound of footsteps in the hallway and then coming closer to my desk. *Wonder who that is?* I stood up and peered over my cubicle. *It's Joe!* I thought, surprised to see him there.

"Hi, Susan," he said sweetly when he got to my desk. "I'm about to step out for a bite at Zio's. Want to join me?" Zio's was a nearby Italian restaurant, a favorite lunch spot for my coworkers and me.

"I do need a break," I said. "So I'd love to join you. I guess I can finish up my paperwork when we get back."

Zio's was such a familiar, friendly place for me that it was easy to let my guard down with Joe. Over a specialty pizza, we shared small talk about our lives, more than we had shared in our typical hallway conversations. Joe looked great in his crisp, dark jeans and V-necked sweater—put together and charming as always, even on a relaxed Saturday afternoon. We laughed and chatted the afternoon away. For the first time, I saw glimpses of a warm and compassionate Joe underneath his polished exterior.

When we returned to work, Joe asked me to stop by his office before heading to mine to check something for him on his computer. Though I don't remember a single detail about the conversation, I vividly remember what happened next.

I sat in his chair looking at his screen. While sitting there, Joe gently put his hand on my shoulder, something so simple, seemingly so innocent. The moment Joe's hand rested on my shoulder, I leaned my head into his arm, almost without realizing it. Those two simple movements changed everything.

Although that Saturday was the first day I let myself admit my attraction to Joe, I still felt compelled to proceed cautiously. I was confused by my own emotions and still very unsure of how to navigate the waters of a budding office romance. *How difficult or awkward will it be at work? Is there really any chance this relationship can work?* I wondered.

Joe was so different from anyone I had ever dated. He was a city boy who had attended college out west. I was a small-town girl from Pennsylvania who had gone to school near home. I was curious, but knowing little about Joe, I tentatively accepted his offer for happy hour drinks on one condition: we drive separately.

A week later, we headed to a bar near work. I ordered a wine cooler, and Joe a beer. The time melted away with our effortless conversation. After a few hours of visiting over drinks and appetizers, I was ready to call it a night.

"Would you like another?" the waitress asked, picking up my empty glass.

"No, thank you," I responded with a smile.

Joe looked up at the waitress and, with a firm voice, said, "Bring her another."

Her face filled with confusion as she looked at me.

"No, thank you," I said again firmly.

Before she could turn and walk away, Joe demanded, "Bring her another. I'm paying, so I decide. Bring us another round."

While I appreciated Joe's generosity, his harshness with the waitress and his apparent need to override my decision made me extremely uncomfortable. An unfamiliar, quiet voice welled up within me, *He just completely ignored you and demanded his own way. How arrogant! How rude! Did you hear how he talked to the waitress? That was wrong. Really wrong!* It was the first time I'd heard that inner whisper, one I would come to know well over the coming years. While I didn't yet recognize it, I couldn't shake the feeling that I should listen to it.

When the waitress brought my drink, I defiantly left it untouched; not so much as one sip passed my lips.

A few minutes later I told Joe it was time to call it a night; we parted ways in the dark parking lot. I slipped into my car, thankful that I had insisted that we drive separately. Perplexed, I headed home unsure of what to make of the evening. Our conversation had been wonderful, warm, and flirtatious. And yet the sour note that ended our night provided a glimmer of a very different Joe, one that I chose to brush aside.

Monday morning at work, I bumped into the charming, dapper Joe. "Hello," he said warmly, smiling gently at me. With that one greeting, I chose to focus on the generous, fun Joe who had dominated our first date.

MY AMERICAN DREAM

After our initial date, Joe and I began spending much of our free time together. Soon contact with Blake dwindled to almost nothing. I never told him about Joe, but somehow I think he knew.

The steady flow of compliments from Joe that had previously caught my attention returned in earnest. He regularly encouraged me with his acclamations and his attention. It wasn't uncommon for Joe to surprise me with flowers or a gift, saying, "I wanted you to know I was thinking about you." I remember once returning from a weekend away. Joe showed up at my apartment with a gift—a sharp new outfit for work: blazer, blouse, skirt, shoes, necklace; he'd thought of everything.

It didn't take long to see that's just how Joe was. Birthdays, Christmases, and other holidays were always spectacular events. Joe spared no expense when spoiling those he cared for. No matter what the holiday or event, I could always count on Joe to deliver the unexpected. From clothes to jewelry, he bought me only the best. That was just who he was. At heart, Joe was incredibly generous. It didn't take long before all of that attention consumed me.

Joe's attention went beyond compliments and material gifts. He took time to show he believed in me, mentoring my professional development. About a year after getting to know Joe, he helped me pursue a job opening at a global technology company. He knew our company offered minimal promotional opportunities and that the new job had great potential. When I was offered the position, he took me out to one of the best restaurants in our area to celebrate.

"I told you that you'd be going places. This is just the start," Joe said, raising his glass to toast me.

"Thank you for helping me with my résumé and helping me get ready for the interview," I said. "I really appreciate everything you've done for me!"

Joe was only too happy to take credit for my new job. "Stick with me. You'll go far," he said smugly.

While we no longer worked for the same company, Joe continued to be very interested in my professional development. My new regional headquarters job was an amazing career opportunity, promising potential future growth. Along the way, Joe helped me refine my professional writing and communication skills. He took an active interest in helping me develop the professional polish that he was so well-known for.

My new organization regularly conducted performance evaluations and merit pay increases based on performance ranking. Disappointed after receiving a lackluster review from my manager, I vented to Joe. "This sounds like I just showed up for work and didn't really do anything extra," I said, disheartened, holding my manager's review out for Joe to see. "I don't understand because when I was still new, I took on all of Anne's work when she went out on maternity leave. Doesn't he remember all of the extra work he gave me?"

"Let me take a look at it and then I'll tell you what we need to do. Remember who I am, who you're dealing with here," Joe said firmly.

For the next few minutes I watched as Joe read through the thin documentation outlining my contributions over the previous year. As he read, his facial expression changed, appearing both thoughtful and calculating. When he was done reading, he sat up straight and cleared his throat.

"This is going to be a piece of cake," he said with booming confidence. "When I'm done with this, you'll have an amazing write-up that you need to take back to him. You'll have to tell him that he needs to rewrite it based on *your* input. And you need to be very firm.

"It's obvious. He didn't take any time writing this. He didn't really consider your contribution to your department at all," Joe continued.

Together we sat down and brainstormed the projects I had worked on. Joe helped me recall and document the impact of my efforts, painting a more accurate portrayal of my performance.

"You need to take all of this to him," Joe said, holding both my initial review and the documentation we had created together. "Tell him that his review is completely unacceptable and that you refuse to sign it. You need to tell him you'll only sign it once he's taken the time to write an accurate and thorough review."

I knew my approach wouldn't be as direct as Joe's, but his coaching helped me gain the confidence to approach my manager.

On Monday morning, I set up a meeting with my manager and provided him with the new documentation for my review. He agreed to take the time to more effectively document my efforts and provide a new evaluation ranking based on more thorough consideration of my work. The result was beyond what I ever would have imagined.

Not only did my manager rewrite my evaluation and increase my raise, he gained a new and greater respect for my work. Over the coming months, I received off-cycle increases as well as promotional opportunities.

Joe had successfully taught me to advocate for myself at work, which caused my manager to notice me. My gratitude translated into affection. Without a doubt, I was falling for Joe.

Though our relationship continued to develop a good foundation, I occasionally began to see ever-so-slight cracks in Joe's well-rounded, sophisticated self. The confidence he conveyed at times came across a bit more like arrogance than self-assurance. But because he continued to succeed due to that very assertiveness, I dismissed my nagging feelings and told myself that I was making a big deal about nothing.

But then glimpses of Joe's jealous nature began to sporadically surface.

My first tangible memory began with a surprise phone call one Saturday evening. Joe and I had just settled in on the couch with a bowl of popcorn at my apartment to watch a movie. The phone rang and I jumped up to grab it. Then I sat back down next to Joe. "Hello, Susan; it's Nelson," the voice on the other end of the phone began. "I hope you don't mind that I found your parents' number and asked them for yours." It was the voice of an old boyfriend from college. The call, out of the blue, was his attempt to reconnect, even if just as friends. Long before the days of Facebook and the ability to simply send a friend request, Nelson had gone out of his way to reconnect. We had parted ways on a friendly note, so it didn't seem odd that he was calling to catch up. That is, until Joe caught wind of who I was talking to.

Joe fumed. "Why is he trying to reconnect with you?" he asked while I tried to listen to both him and Nelson. "Tell him you're in a relationship and aren't interested. He has no business calling you if it's over between you."

He paused while I tried to hear what Nelson was saying. "Tell him! Your dad should never have given anyone your number."

I don't remember the exact words I relayed to Nelson on the phone that night, but I do know that with them, I ended a friendship with an old college friend. Loyal to Joe, I didn't want contact with an old boyfriend to damage our relationship.

That was just the first of many such conversations. Over several months, I let go of nearly all of my guy friendships because they seemed to make Joe uncomfortable. I declined the near weekly invitations from coworkers heading out for happy hour, even if it was an all-girl group. I found excuses not to participate in fun events, such as seasonal outings to ball games or the popular yearly outing to the nearby horse races at the Preakness Stakes. I wasn't sure Joe would get along with my coworkers and friends, so I felt uncomfortable inviting him. And I knew if I wanted to go without him, it would only bring stress to our relationship. I was desperate to prove my loyalty to Joe. Holding on to what I believed was real love was more important to me than anything else. Looking back, I realize now that I was disillusioned—thinking I was at the stage in life when I was supposed to find love and live happily ever after. *If I let my chance at love slip away, what might that mean for my future?* I had wondered.

I longed to protect Joe's sense of security; I slowly let other friendships slip away one by one. I didn't consciously choose to let them go. Instead, it was the natural consequence to the many declined invitations over time. Eventually, coworkers and friends stopped asking. Bit by bit, I began letting go of pieces of myself along the way, but I couldn't see it. I don't think anyone else noticed either. They just assumed I was investing in my relationship. Not until years later did a few family members and friends admit that while they saw changes, they didn't know what, if anything, they should say or do about their observations.

About a year into my relationship with Joe, I regrettably destroyed one of my most treasured relationships: my friendship with Blake. It was early one evening. Joe and I had just finished cleaning up the dinner dishes when the phone rang. I picked up. It was Blake. His voice quivered as he told me that his mother had passed away.

"I'm so sorry," I replied, trying to provide some comfort.

"Will you travel to the funeral with me?" Blake asked.

I knew how close Blake had been to his mom. I desperately wanted to go.

Looking at Joe, who was trying to figure out what was going on, I mouthed words to explain the situation. "Could you hold on a second, Blake?" I said. I covered the mouthpiece to talk to Joe.

"If you go, it's over," Joe asserted. "If you can travel that far away with another guy, it's over. You can't be loyal to me and be that type of support for someone else. It won't work."

In a heartbreaking instant, I looked at Joe standing in front of me and then down at the phone in my hand. Over the months, he had doted on me. He had pursued me. He had mentored me, helping me attain career growth. I *knew* he cared about me. Blake, on the other hand, hadn't fought for me. In fact, he had all but stopped calling. My hopes that anything could ever work out with him seemed like nothing but a distant dream.

In that moment, as I was forced into a decision, I told Blake I was so sorry but I couldn't attend the funeral with him. It was the last time I ever talked to Blake.

To this day, I regret my lack of support for a friend I truly treasured. I let fear rule my actions, and I lost sight of what really mattered. I hadn't yet realized that love and fear are not synonymous. Love ruled by fear is not really love at all—a lesson learned through many very difficult years.

I now see how Joe carefully manipulated me into letting go of my friends. I was too naive to notice at the time and most definitely did not understand the implications. I mistook Joe's attention for genuine caring, for true love. I thought, *He must really and sincerely love me to pursue me so intently.* While I believe Joe did love me, at the time I did not realize that his definition of love was not a healthy, nurturing love but a controlling and manipulative love. I discounted his arrogance, calling it confidence. I dismissed his jealousy, deeming it love. I accepted his ultimatums, trusting that he wanted only the best for me. Longing to be loved, to have someone of my own, superseded my common sense and clouded my youthful judgment.

Over the next three years, Joe continued to use his charm, polish, and debonair style to woo me. He pampered me for the most part. We dined at our favorite local restaurants, took in concerts under the stars at a nearby amphitheater, and walked the same beachside boardwalk that I had once walked with Blake. In return, Joe asked for little, except for one thing: loyalty.

To me, loyalty in a relationship was a given. It was a quality that seemed naturally to be at the foundation of our relationship. Eventually, I would learn that for Joe, anything that made him uncomfortable, insecure, jealous—whether warranted or not—challenged his trust of my loyalty. Still, I never imagined he would purposefully set out to test me just to see if I could reach the depth of loyalty he required.

One evening after work, I stopped by Joe's apartment. I knocked and walked in as I had so many other times. Stepping into the apartment, I immediately sensed a somber tone. Joe didn't look up immediately or greet me the way he usually did. Instead, he slowly looked up from his slouched position on the couch. "Oh, hi there," he said, his voice heavy, wavering. It almost sounded as though he were choking back tears.

"What's wrong?" I asked, immediately concerned by the very different Joe I saw sitting there. His normal confident smile was replaced with a look of insecurity.

"Come sit down," he said, lightly patting the place next to him, his voice still trembling.

"Joe, what's wrong?" I repeated as I sat beside him.

His eyes slowly lifted to meet mine, locking for a long lingering moment before his focus returned to the floor in front of the couch. His eyes were filled with sadness and a sense of pain that I had never seen in him before.

"Joe, you're scaring me. What's wrong?" I said, inching closer to him.

"Susan, I'm moving." His voice quivered. "To Denver," he added, his voice trailing off.

"What? No! Why?" I spat out, trying to make sense of this abrupt news. What was he thinking? How could he just uproot and leave after all this time? I was truly at a loss. "Joe, why?!" I repeated. My words hung in the air. Sitting in silence for that long, lingering moment, I felt time stand still. Tears began streaming down my cheeks, dropping onto the couch between us.

Joe reached up with his hand and tenderly wiped my tears away. "Don't cry," he said softly, pulling me closer.

I looked up, trying to focus on Joe through a puddle of tears. "Joe, why?"

"I need to move home," Joe began. "My job here is shifting. I found out today that our contract didn't get renewed. It's only a matter of time until they'll be letting my department go."

"Joe, you can get another job here."

"It's not just about work," Joe continued. "My mom is going through some really difficult challenges. I really need to move back." His words hit my heart like a brick. I lost my struggle to contain my tears and began sobbing.

"Oh, Susan," Joe said tenderly. "I hate to see you cry." He continued to softly wipe the tears from my cheek. His hand paused to cradle my face as he leaned forward and gently kissed my forehead.

"But what's going to happen to us? Why do you have to move?" I blurted out between my tears.

"You're not going to get rid of me that easily," Joe said with a slight smile. "We *will* stay in touch."

"Joe, you're moving halfway across the country. It won't be the same," I cried out. "Why do you have to move? *Please* don't move!" I begged.

Joe pulled me closer and wrapped his arms around me. Together we collapsed into the corner of his oversized couch.

"I promise, I *will* stay in touch. You'll still hear from me," Joe said reassuringly.

"It won't be the same!" I said, looking up at Joe.

"I'll do my best to stay in touch, but you're probably right; things will be different."

"Isn't there anything you can do? Do you have to move?"

We hugged and cried together. And I begged.

"I'll see what I can do," Joe offered. "I'll see what I can come up with to help my mom from here. I can't promise, but I'll try."

Joe gave me a squeeze and kissed my forehead again. "You know it means the world to me to know you care so much."

My heart filled with sadness and a deep ache. It was only lessened by knowing that Joe was touched by my emotion. Consumed by this new development, a sense of impending loss weighed heavily upon me. I sincerely believed Joe's planned move would tear apart our relationship.

One day several years later, Joe and I were reminiscing about our early days together. He brought up that evening. And then, shocking me, he confessed that it had all been part of an elaborate ruse designed to test and solidify my loyalty. It had worked, because threatened with the chance of losing Joe and having to step forward in life alone, I found myself looking past our challenges. I had genuinely begged him not to leave. But, in reality, Joe had *never* had any plans to move at all. *That emotional night was just part of a charade?* I thought angrily. *How could he do that?*

Seeing the look on my face, he explained what he had been feeling, and I believed him. "I love you, Susan. I really, truly love you," Joe said. "I'm so sorry what I put you through that night. I never intended to hurt you. I just needed to know where I stood with you."

I sat silently hanging on to each word Joe spoke as though my next breath depended upon it.

"I've fallen for you. I think about you day and night. I can't imagine my life without you," Joe continued. "I just needed to know if you felt the same way. I love you." I believed every carefully, emotionally confessed word that hung in the air.

We never again talked about that night. For that matter, we never really talked about that night or any other differences because I didn't want to upset Joe. I let any form of conflict quietly fade away. I didn't want him to doubt that I cared. I found that if I didn't give Joe reason to doubt my loyalty, life seemed good. In fact, I believed life *was* good.

Then one evening, my dream came true! Joe proposed. And boy did he go all out. "I want only the best for you, Susan," he told me lovingly. He spared no expense. Only after researching what makes a diamond superior did he select a brilliant sparkling solitaire diamond engagement ring. He showered me with a large, beautiful bouquet of flowers, and we celebrated at one of our favorite restaurants. I was consumed with excitement. Childhood dreams of the perfect wedding distracted me while I was at work. At home I eagerly flipped through bridal magazines, searching for ideas that would make our day perfect.

But regardless of my initial bliss, over the several months of our engagement, a gnawing, uneasy feeling periodically washed over me. *It must just be cold feet,* I told myself. Some days the feeling was more intense. At home, Joe and I spent most of our free time together, leaving me little time to reflect and understand my unexpected doubt.

Still, beneath my confident exterior, a small voice of uncertainty remained at my core. One Saturday while participating in a professional development class in Washington, DC, I became distracted by my tentative thoughts. During one break, I lingered in the lobby outside of the conference room, seeking to regain my focus on the day ahead. Glancing up, I saw a pay phone on the far side of the lobby. *I need to call Blake*, I told myself. If I could talk to him, maybe I could discern my feelings. I knew I could talk through my concerns with him and find clarity. My hand trembled as I dialed his number. My heart raced when the phone began to ring. I hadn't spoken with him since the difficult conversation we'd had when his mother died. While the phone rang, I rehearsed excitedly in my mind, *"Hi Blake; it's Susan."* *What will he think about this call from out of the blue?* I wondered. As the phone continued to ring, I tried to find just the right words to say. Then Blake's answering machine clicked on.

"Hi, this is Blake," I heard in his bright voice. "I can't come to the phone right now, so please leave a message and I'll get back to you." My heart sank as I placed the receiver back on the hook. *It must be a sign*, I reassured myself. I returned to the seminar convinced that I needed to put all doubts aside. My focus shifted from my concerns to planning a beautiful wedding day.

Our weekend wedding was set for a lovely, early fall day in my hometown in Pennsylvania. Joe and I, along with our friends and family, came together for a spectacular weekend. The night before our wedding, I met Sam, Joe's dad, for the first time.

During the weeks leading up to our wedding, Joe wasn't even sure if he wanted to invite Sam. They hadn't really had a relationship in years. Joe admitted that he hadn't forgiven his dad for the world of hurt he'd brought into Joe's life when he was young. He hated that Sam was an alcoholic who cheated on his mom. He hated that his parents divorced as he attempted to navigate the awkward years of adolescence. But most of all, he hated the memories that scarred his childhood years, memories of abuse at his father's hand.

I really couldn't comprehend the broken family life Joe described. His stories were completely foreign to me. I had no experience to compare it to. Having come from a very loving family, I hoped Joe and Sam could find healing, a sense of common ground, and reconcile. Joe hoped for the same.

Following our rehearsal dinner, Joe, Sam, and several male relatives headed to a local bar for a late-night of conversation. The night provided the beginnings of a foundation between Sam and Joe. It brought a sense of peace to Joe for which I was grateful as we stepped into our new married life.

Our wedding day was all that I had dreamed it would be. My father walked me down the aisle of the church we had attended when I was young. Joe and I continued our romantic story with a magnificent seven-day honeymoon in Hawaii. Yes, life was good.

You might think that Joe came from money the way he so effortlessly spent it on me as well as others. Instead, the opposite was true. After his parents went through their difficult divorce, Joe's mother did what she could to make ends meet. They didn't have the extras in life, and went without anything that wasn't truly a necessity. As an adult, Joe went out of his way to enjoy those "extras" as well as provide for others wherever he saw the opportunity to make a difference or bring an unexpected smile. Once we were married, it didn't take long for Joe's generosity to extend to my family.

One late summer day, Joe helped me make a dream experience come true for my dad. Having grown up in central Pennsylvania, my parents and entire family had always been avid Penn State fans, regularly cheering on the Nittany Lions at home football games. While we often tailgated, we couldn't help but notice the elaborate tailgate spreads hosted by the RVs parked near the stadium. "One day I'd like to do that," my father had said on more than one occasion. "One day."

A few years into our marriage, Joe and I searched for ideas for a birthday gift for my father. Our thoughts drifted back to my father's "one day." Together, we decided to rent an RV for a weekend to give my father the gift of the experience he had always hoped for. It was far more than we'd typically spend on a gift, but Joe made it happen. If something was important to someone Joe cared about, his generosity knew no bounds.

Joe's support for others was more than financial; he genuinely cared about their emotional well-being too. One year, a family member was devastated to find that her husband had had an affair with a close friend. The truth unfolded before her when she stumbled upon a box of recent love letters he had kept. While Joe and I were both appalled, it hit a deep nerve within him.

"How could he do that?" Joe said bitterly. "How could anyone betray his wife like that? And his children? I thought he was a better man than that."

"It just doesn't make any sense. Everything seemed to be going so well for them," I responded.

"There are no words to describe someone who'd stoop so low. This whole situation is so unnecessary." His words were full of empathy and pain. "I will *never* put you through anything like this, *ever*! I know what it's like to be on the other side of this," Joe said firmly. "When my father left my mother, I watched my family fall apart. This is just terrible."

As Joe continued, emotion and pain washed over his face. His eyes glistened with tears. It was as though his entire being became engulfed with the hurt and emotions he felt from our relative's recent betrayal coupled with his parents' long-ago divorce. He had seen firsthand as a young child the devastation affairs could cause. His words couldn't seem to fully capture his disgust for the situation.

"I could never put you through something like this!" Joe said adamantly. "*Never.*"

I pulled Joe close and gave him a long hug. "Joe, you have nothing to worry about with me. I'll never put you through anything like this either. I feel so bad for her, for the kids."

Joe kissed me on the cheek. We lingered, standing with our arms around each other, comforting each other. We felt reassured in our own marriage, thankful that we were both fully committed to each other.

Two years into our marriage brought more blessings. Our home dynamic shifted as we welcomed our daughter Jennifer. It was a wonderful chapter of our marriage—in fact, it was the start of several fantastic chapters. Together, Joe and I painted and furnished our Winnie the Pooh-themed nursery. We bought a beautiful crib with a matching changing table. Wanting to make the nursery our own, I painted a series of pictures that retold a Pooh story.

It was a magical time. Together we began navigating life as proud new parents. Joe quickly became involved in helping with our new bundle of joy. He eagerly worked to establish his definition of the role of a father without having his own positive memories to draw upon.

While he wasn't the quickest to change a diaper, he was quick to hold Jennifer or help give her a bottle. He also loved making her laugh, which brought joy to all of us. Despite not having his own role model, Joe was a proud new dad, and he tried to be the best dad he could be.

Life settled into a typical new-parent routine. We rarely got enough sleep, but somehow we found the energy to make it through. Typical of our suburb, our little sidewalk-lined cul-de-sac provided a great place for walks together, our daughter beaming in her stroller. In the summer, our townhouse's postage-stamp-sized backyard was big enough for the addition of a small wading pool. Who knew that six inches of water could bring so much joy and laughter? Our small family soaked in the warmth of the summer and hosted more than one crab feast in our backyard. I treasure the pictures of Jennifer sitting on my lap, a contagious smile on her precious face. Joe too was touched by our tender family moments. The closeness these times brought were bittersweet for Joe. While he loved what was unfolding for our young family, he couldn't keep his own memories of a troubled childhood at bay. He began sharing stories from his painful past. As a young boy, he had hungered for time with his dad. One day as his father began getting ready to leave to go somewhere, he asked Joe if he wanted to go along. Overwhelmed with excitement and joy, Joe enthusiastically responded, "Yes!"

"Then go get your coat and shoes, son," Sam replied.

Joe darted upstairs, grabbed his shoes, and laced them as fast as he could. Not slowing down long enough to put his coat on, he reached his arms around trying to catch the sleeves as he bounded down the stairs. When Joe hit the landing in the middle of the stairs, he was startled by the sound of the front door closing. He ran down the rest of the stairs and bolted over to the front window. With a swift motion he moved the curtain out of the way just in time to see his father get in the car and leave. His heart broke as he longingly stared out the window in disbelief. Being deliberately left by his father that day tormented Joe for years to come.

As painful as the aloneness had been for Joe on that difficult day, there were many other heart-wrenching stories of beatings and being locked in a dark closet or attic. One day, he and his siblings stood in the kitchen enjoying an after-school snack. They joked and talked, enjoying their few minutes of downtime before they planned to start their homework. As they finished their snacks, their jovial fun was interrupted by the sound of approaching footsteps outside. They knew they were supposed to start their homework right way after school and feared being punished. Hoping to flee before being caught, they all turned to scatter when one of his sisters bumped a glass on the counter. With a loud crash, the glass shattered, spraying shards of glass across the kitchen just as the front door opened.

In an instant, they knew their clean getaway had shattered along with the glass.

"What's going on here?" Sam boomed. Joe and his siblings trembled in fear.

"It was me," Joe said, knowing that whatever followed would not be good. Although he hadn't bumped the glass, he decided he would rather take the punishment than witness his sister endure it. Joe remembered enduring one of the worst beatings of his childhood that harrowing afternoon. After an awful whipping, he was locked in the attic for hours. Even after all the years since that dreadful day, Joe's words still dripped with pain and raw emotion when he talked about it.

The difficulties of Joe's past brought us closer as we cherished our new roles as parents. We both wanted the best care for Jennifer once I returned to work. Concerned about how much attention she might get in a traditional day care setting, we decided instead to opt for a live-in au pair. The idea of hosting someone from overseas was natural to me. As I grew up, my family had hosted a number of exchange students. Additionally, I had studied as an exchange student in Sweden. Realizing the positive influence of those experiences in my life, I welcomed the idea of bringing another culture into our home to enrich our family's life. Through a large agency, we found that it would be cost-effective to have an au pair as live-in day care. We also both liked the idea of being able to see our care provider around Jennifer more frequently than a traditional setting would have allowed. We felt reassured that we would be able to pick up on any issues that could arise sooner than we would have otherwise.

Around the time we celebrated Jennifer's first birthday, we received the wonderful news that we were expecting again. We were thrilled the summer would bring another addition to our growing family. Still settling into life as parents, we looked forward to welcoming a new member.

I was completely taken by surprise then, when Joe and I had our first serious argument. Previously, I had successfully managed to keep Joe from getting upset. But this incident made me begin to question our future as a family. On a Saturday afternoon, Jennifer lay on our queen-sized bed. I turned to grab something for her, and as I did, she rolled off. Our bed, very low to the ground, wasn't much of a danger; however, Jennifer was surprised and began screaming earnestly, getting the attention of Joe, who was downstairs. As he rushed through the bedroom door to see what was wrong, he didn't care that Jennifer was unharmed or that I was soothing her.

"You are incompetent!" Joe shouted when he found out that she'd rolled off the bed. "What are you doing?"

"Joe, she's fine. She just rolled over. She's not hurt," I said cradling Jennifer.

"You are completely useless. How could you let that happen?"

"She's okay," I said, trying to reassure Joe.

"You don't get it do you? You don't even know when you've put your own daughter in harm's way. You really are useless," Joe snapped.

I didn't respond. I didn't dare respond. It seemed that anything I said only fueled Joe's anger. Instead, I stood paralyzed, numb and shocked at Joe's cruel outburst. But my silence didn't stop Joe either.

"You are more than useless; you are unfit to be a mother!" Joe yelled. "You have no right to raise children, and definitely have no business raising my children. Mark my words, I will divorce you and take my daughter and our unborn child from you as soon as you deliver. You will NOT raise them! You are unfit to be a mother!"

I was completely at a loss. While I could understand his concern, the depth of Joe's anger shocked me. *Divorce? Would he really go there? Would he really take my children from me?* I thought as Joe continued to berate my parenting skills. Had I become the enemy? I was just a tired mom doing the best I could.

In disgust, Joe stormed out of the room and retreated downstairs while I remained upstairs with Jennifer. In complete disbelief, I collapsed into our oversized rocking chair with my precious daughter. Tears welled in my eyes as we rocked, but as I comforted my daughter, I found a semblance of peace.

How could Joe so easily suggest divorce from out of nowhere? I continued to wonder. When we got married we had agreed we were committed to each other for better or worse. How could his commitment so easily change with the tears of a child?

I remained upstairs until I was certain Joe's anger had subsided. When I finally did gain the courage to join him downstairs much later, I pretended that his outburst had never happened. We never revisited the situation or talked through the tornado of emotion that had torn through our home that afternoon.

Although there were no visible signs of the destruction Joe's outburst had caused during the following days and weeks, our marriage was never the same after that. Joe's threat of divorce had shaken me to the core. Where was the man who had vowed he was committed to our marriage? How could I ensure that our daughter would never fall, never get hurt, or cry? Would Joe react this way whenever she became upset? I tried to be the best mom I could be, taking the best possible care of our daughter while trying to be the best wife I could be. If I just did enough, tried hard enough, was careful enough, maybe I could avoid another explosion, I reasoned.

But several weeks later I unsuspectingly walked into a surprise encounter with Joe's anger. On that particular day, Joe made it home from work before I did. "How was your day?" I innocently asked as I walked into our kitchen.

"Where were you?" Joe asked harshly without acknowledging that I'd spoken.

"At work," I said, not really understanding his question. *He knows I was at work*, I thought, puzzled.

"After work, where did you go?" Joe asked.

"I came straight home, why?"

"No you didn't," he said as his eyes met mine with a cold stare. "I left work early and I saw you. I was behind you coming across Willow and then you turned onto Jones Road about an hour ago. Where did you go?"

"Joe, I have no idea what you're talking about. I left work twenty minutes ago, and I'm here now."

"I *saw* you, Susan."

"I seriously have no idea what you're talking about," I said. "I was at work!"

"I was behind your van. I saw you."

Our frustrating conversation spiraled downward as Joe's anger deepened. Convinced that he'd seen my van in front of him, Joe was not open to another explanation despite the fact that in our suburb blue Dodge Caravans seemed to be the most popular vehicle that year. I could think of absolutely no way to defend myself. The wave of paranoia and insecurity that consumed Joe left no room for discussion.

With no clear way to resolve the situation, both still angry, we swept it under the rug, adding to the growing mound of our unresolved issues. Something we would do often in the future.

I quickly learned that Joe's paranoia extended beyond his concern for my loyalty. Periodically if a car would drive slowly down our street, Joe would watch with careful interest.

"Joe, they're probably just looking for an address," I typically offered. But he insisted on watching until the situation resolved by the car's either leaving the neighborhood or turning into a driveway. The periodic wrong phone call seemed to place Joe into a temporary alert status — watching, listening, ready to defend our family, our home. From what, I'm not exactly sure, but he professed to be ever ready.

Around the same time, Joe came home with a handgun from a local gun show.

"Joe, I don't want that in the house," I said, not thrilled to have another gun in our house. Joe already owned a shotgun that he too often left leaning in our front closet, loaded.

"I'll keep it out of reach," Joe said, attempting to reassure me.

"Did you get a case for it?" I asked, hoping he would put in place some consideration to keep our children safe.

"No, but I promise I will," he said, compromising. The next weekend he purchased a locking case and kept his new firearm safely locked away. It took quite a bit more convincing for him to move his shotgun. Eventually, he locked that away as well. And with that, Joe's paranoia and deep-seated anger went into hibernation for many months to come.

Several months later, we welcomed with great excitement the arrival of our second child, Ryan. From the start, he was a content baby, whom we smothered with love. It was sweet to see how Jennifer quickly stepped into the role of big sister and loved doing anything she could to help her little brother. Joe also adapted to his extended role as Dad and was happy to play with our children and even help feed them. Our two young children soon became energetic toddlers before our eyes. We loved every minute and took the kids to the park, the zoo, or to the beach. Looking back, our early years were packed full, bursting with wonderful memories sprinkled with shared, tender parenting moments.

One particular night is vividly etched in my memory. Every parent has those days that pose an extra challenge. Unfortunately, Joe and I weren't immune. On that particular day, Jennifer just hadn't been herself. During the evening, she became increasingly restless and fussy. Nothing soothed her. Desperate to find some way to comfort her, we decided to let her curl up in our bed. It seemed to work well, the three of us quickly drifting off to sleep. Some time later we were startled awake by our bed's shaking and were horrified to realize the source was our little Jennifer... convulsing on the bed between us. I scooped my arms under our precious toddler to cradle her. Her small body radiated incredible heat.

"Joe, she's burning up! She's really hot!"

Joe jumped out of bed and grabbed a thermometer and a wet washcloth from our bathroom. I put the cloth across her forehead while I took her temperature. First with concern and then panic, I watched the thermometer climb: 101, 101.5, 102, 102.5, 103, 103.5,104.

"Joe, it's already at 104! And it's still going!"

I continued to watch the reading climb: 104.2, 104.4, 104.6. *Beep, beep, beep,* the thermometer chirped at 104.6 degrees—dangerously high. We stared helplessly at our precious daughter's quivering body. We knew we needed to rush her to the emergency room.

We left Ryan home with our au pair, asleep in his crib, completely unaware of the unfolding drama. Upon arrival at the emergency room, we were immediately taken into an examining room. Jennifer's body no longer trembled as it had earlier. Instead, I carried her seemingly lifeless body draped over my arms, like a life-sized rag doll, her arms and legs limp.

A nurse swooped in and began to assess Jennifer. I was instructed to place her on the large hospital bed to prevent my body temperature from keeping hers elevated. As I laid her down, my eyes met her sweet, innocent eyes. Those large, brown, empty eyes stared back at me almost as if to ask for help.

"105.9," the attending nurse said to an emergency room medic who joined us in the room. In the twenty minutes since taking Jennifer's temperature at home until arriving in the ER, her temperature had climbed another 1.3 degrees. My heart broke; I was helpless to aid my little girl. Together with Joe, I waited for her fever to break, for the hospital personnel to help our cherished daughter.

"It's going to be okay, sweetie," Joe said to her, his voice trembling.

"Mommy and Daddy are here," I said, trying to offer comfort with my words though I longed to hold her.

A short time later Jennifer began to respond to the medication they had given her, fidgeting a bit while her eyes came to life. She looked up, fixing her eyes on the oversized blood pressure dial mounted near her bed. "Clock," she said in her sweet, young voice. Tears welled in my eyes. She was back.

Joe and I—together—endured a very scary, tender night at the bedside of our very sick daughter, a memory full of compassion, caring, but most of all love.

We shared countless other memories filled with warmth and love. Some of our best memories were the holidays, when Joe showed his love through his generosity. Through his joy and excitement, he became a kid again. In the fall, we brought home the largest pumpkins we could find—as big as our children. At Christmastime, we brought home the biggest tree on the lot. Joe loved spoiling Jennifer and Ryan with piles of presents under the tree. He consistently spoiled me too and also found ways to make Christmas enjoyable for his family, sending giant boxes home to his mother, sisters, nieces, and nephews each year.

During those early years of our marriage, Joe was regularly consumed with generosity. Occasionally though, through the course of daily life, something out of the blue would ignite his fuse and his anger would rage. In the beginning, these flare-ups were few and far between. Life would quickly return to our normal routine as a happy family. The kind, generous Joe would return. His change was so convincing each time that I was left believing the change was permanent and life would remain peaceful.

CRACKS IN THE FOUNDATION

As part of our family's routine, each year we welcomed a new au pair. Most definitely, the biggest downside of using au pairs for our childcare was the requirement that we needed to find a new one each year. The visas issued to au pairs prevented them from staying any longer. While the large agency we used made the process somewhat easy, it still required an adjustment and transition every time. Sarah, our third au pair, joined our family not long before Ryan's first birthday. She was a quiet, demure, maybe even a little awkward, eighteen-year-old when she arrived. Within just a few weeks, she became like a sister to us, an aunt to our children. Although she was technically off duty on weekends, Sarah often joined us on our family outings. From our town's Fourth of July celebration to our weeklong family beach vacation, she became an integral part of our young family.

At this point in my career I didn't often travel for work; however, the occasional opportunity did arise. During Sarah's year, I had the unique opportunity to travel to Cape May, New Jersey. My team's manager planned a two-day retreat in the charming Victorian coastal town just a few hours away. He negotiated a great nightly rate at a beautiful bed-and-breakfast near the beach. My team's recent focus on several critical deliverables made such a team-building retreat sound like a breath of fresh air.

"You're not going," Joe said when I told him about my need to travel.

"Joe, my entire team is going. I need to go," I said.

"I know how these things work," Joe said. "It's not about work at all. You aren't going."

"I need to go. My entire team is going," I said, repeating myself.

Even the thought of such a trip brought incredible stress to our relationship. Internally I was conflicted. I didn't want to upset Joe; however, I was part of a professional team with work obligations. The situation hung over me like a dense, black cloud; I was desperate to find a resolution. It was Joe who finally suggested a compromise.

"You can go if you take Sarah and the kids with you," he said with a tinge of pride in his voice. Looking back, it was classic Joe. He created the problem and then expected tremendous accolades upon offering a solution. But this, like many of Joe's solutions, always came with a twist. Yes, I could travel to Cape May, but staying at a pristine Victorian bed-and-breakfast with two toddlers clearly wouldn't work.

"I guess you'll have to find someplace else to stay," Joe said leaving me to navigate the limitations of his compromise. Despite my entire team's staying at the same place, I needed to find a kid-friendly option nearby. Joe expected me to be both thrilled and thankful for his wonderful idea. Instead, it left me feeling less than, unequal to my peers at work. Sure, I was an adult, but I didn't have "permission" to participate fully in my work retreat.

When it was time for the trip, many of my coworkers carpooled to New Jersey. Instead I packed up my two toddlers, Sarah, a Pack 'n Play, a double stroller, and enough entertainment for our crew for the few days we'd be away. I did my best to keep a positive attitude, trying to spin the trip as a minivacation with work built in.

During the retreat, Joe called often. He insisted that I check in with him on breaks and let him know when I would be returning to the hotel room with Sarah and our children. The first day of activity was topped off with a team-building dinner cruise in the evening. It truly offered an escape for all of the senses. Standing on the deck, I closed my eyes for a moment and inhaled a long, slow breath. Salty air and a soft breeze—unmistakable reminders that despite being only a few hours from home, I was in a completely different world. Opening my eyes, I focused on a flock of seagulls swooping by our boat, their calls seeming to laugh as they sailed by. The sky was streaked with brilliant shades of pink and orange, the beginnings of what soon would be a breathtaking sunset. My momentary respite, my opportunity to soak in the beautiful summer evening and the stunning coastline, my enjoyment—all was shattered by Joe's relentless calling. Every few minutes, it seemed, my cell phone would ring. He wasn't just calling to say hi. Instead, every call was peppered with his judgmental accusations and constant guilt trips. At the time, I thought Joe's "compromise" had come out of his fear of being left at home and responsible for our children while I traveled. Looking back, I'm sure that wasn't his only motivation. Instead, I think it was a desperate attempt to assert control over my life because he questioned my faithfulness and loyalty. I truly believe his actions were driven by his own insecurity—insecurity that consumed him. Still haunted by the impact of growing up in a home torn apart by the betrayal of an affair, he projected his unresolved pain and fears onto me.

Joe's "compromise" had spoiled my work retreat. But he couldn't spoil everything about work. Actually, the very act of going to work was a bit of a daily retreat for me—a refuge from Joe. No longer at the same company as Joe, I developed a few friendships with peers—a welcomed addition to my world. Cherie was one such friend. While we had started working at the company around the same time, we worked on different teams and didn't meet until the offices within our building were shuffled, locating our offices near one another. It was refreshing to build a friendship outside of Joe's control and influence. However, because of the demands of my life and Joe's jealousy, I typically only got together with friends like Cherie during the workday. Lunchtime meetings were far easier than evening or weekend plans.

Between work and home, our family kept busy and time seemed to melt away. The balance of Sarah's year quickly flew by. With trips to the zoo or vacations to the beach, Joe and I seemed to have successfully navigated from contentious times to more peaceful times—Joe's anger for the most part in hibernation. I couldn't help but wonder if some of our home's new peace was a result of Joe allowing himself to be more fully consumed by his work. He often worked long days or brought work home to complete at night. Although he seemed a bit more withdrawn and distant, I welcomed the increased calm in our home.

The peacefulness of our home was interrupted by the arrival of a few temporary house guests. As Sarah's year came to a close, her parents and brothers came to visit. With each au pair becoming part of our family, we welcomed the opportunity to host our new extended family. Although we lived in just a three-bedroom townhouse, the finished basement offered just enough space to accommodate our visitors. During their stay Sarah planned to take a few days off to travel, then work a few other days while her family took in the local sights.

On one of Sarah's working days, I headed to the office like so many other days during her year with us. Her family lingered, getting ready for their day of adventure. Around 9:00 AM, before my workday could start in earnest, my office phone rang.

"There's been an accident," Sarah said with a trembling voice. "Jennifer and my brothers were running through the basement and Jennifer tripped." Sarah paused. I gasped as a knot quickly formed in the pit of my stomach.

"She hit her head on the corner of the desk," she said. "She's definitely going to need stitches. She's bleeding a lot."

A million questions flooded my mind: *Is she ok? Why were they running in the house? Where were you?* But I knew the immediate need was for me to get home and get Jennifer medical attention as soon as possible. Following a quick call to our pediatrician, we were referred to a plastic surgeon. The gash on her forehead would need careful suturing.

I rushed home, picked up Jennifer, and took her to the surgeon's office. I held a large bandage against her cut while we sat in the waiting room before her name was called.

The nurse ushered us into the small treatment room. "Let's take a look at what we have," she said, lifting the corner of the bandage I still held in place on Jennifer's head. I glanced down at the gash, but quickly needed to look away, my stomach now turning. The nurse must have seen the color drain from my face because she said, "We'll get this cleaned right up. Don't worry, she's only three. She won't remember this at all."

She won't remember this at all? I thought. I held my dear daughter. *Oh, how I wish I could believe that.* I remembered only too well the first time I needed stitches when I was just three. I still remembered falling and the traumatic trip to the doctor's office that followed. I was relieved when the nurse finished quickly.

When Jennifer and I finally got back home, everyone seemed a bit awkward about the events of the day. I learned that while Jennifer and Sarah's brothers ran through our house, Sarah was helping her father figure out our TV and the remote. Understandably, they must all have been mortified. And although I knew what had happened was an accident, I was surprised that no apology was ever offered. Despite the draining events of the day, to all others in my house including Joe, it was as though nothing had happened. The wonderfully tender support I had felt when Joe and I took our feverish daughter to the ER was nowhere to be found. Where was the concerned father who had been ready to take our baby from me because she fell off the bed, or the dad who stayed up all night in the ER with our sick little girl? Weary, I did my best to spend extra time with Jennifer, but I still found myself preparing dinner for a house full of company without the benefit of help from anyone.

Just as I had recognized a change in Joe's supportiveness, I also saw more of Joe's "protective" side, as he called it. He monitored my whereabouts and my plans, peppering me with more questions than a parent might ask a teenager borrowing the car. He also calculated the time necessary to run typical errands. If I were heading to the grocery store and to get gas, even if I didn't say when I might be home, he anticipated.

If I came home later than his calculated time, he was waiting. He was extremely jealous and paranoid—a dangerous combination.

During this season of my life, my work occasionally required travel to California, which only added fuel to Joe's anxiety. My trips were short, but the days were very long. While I was gone, Joe called frequently. In the evenings I typically joined my coworkers for dinner before ending our marathon days. He called and questioned me about who I was meeting. "What's his name?" he would demand. He harassed me with endless questions, grasping to find a basis for his unfounded suspicions. "It's not that you would actually have to cheat on me," Joe would say on countless occasions. "I just need to think you could."

"But, Joe, I would never do that," I'd protest.

Soon, not wanting to let him have even the slightest fear that I'd cheat on him, since that was all it would take for him to get angry, I became limited in my daily life and controlled by his paranoia. Over time, I began to decline many of the dinners with my coworkers because the badgering became unbearable. Instead, I'd opt for a room-service dinner alone in my hotel room, hoping to ease Joe's insecurities. Unfortunately, it only grew worse. My lonely, antisocial dinners were bombarded with the same accusatory questions. Joe fueled his own paranoia, convinced I had shared dinner with someone else in my hotel room. I could do nothing to ease his fear.

The more challenging life became, the more I valued simple things that provided any sense of normalcy or brought levity to my day. One small example was the radio program and its DJs who had previously shared my regular commute. Granted, their jokes weren't always the best, but I remembered countless times of laughing on my way to work. It was always fun to catch myself when I realized I was at a traffic light and the other commuters had no idea why I was laughing so hard. If I wasn't laughing, I was singing along at the top of my lungs. But even this area of my life wasn't problem free.

Out of the blue, the radio station was bought and the old programming discontinued. Overnight, the DJs who had shared my commute were gone. Gone were their bad jokes that had brought levity to my tumultuous world. The music, format, and direction of the station drastically shifted from a top-hits-of-the-day station to a Christian-owned part-talk, part-Christian-music station. This new station, such a radical shift, was foreign to me. Sure, I had grown up going to church on Sundays, but I hadn't really gone to church since I left home to go to college. I had happy memories of Sunday school, church pageants, and even youth group. But to me, religion was something you practiced at 10:30 AM on Sundays. Consequently, I had no desire to make this new station my radio home. I had never before heard the music they played, and their talk show hosts were completely unknown to me. I'll be honest—I resented their taking my commuting companions from me. I wondered who these people were who had snatched up the familiar home on my radio dial.

After the changeover, I occasionally listened to the programs out of curiosity, as though peering into someone else's world. At first I listened for a few minutes, trying to understand who had disbanded my previous commuting companions. But over time, I found I listened for more of my commute. Eventually, I left the station on for the entire drive. I found myself mysteriously intrigued. I had never before heard stories about God that seemed so current, so real. It was long before I would hear of "searching for purple cows," or understand how the things I focus on impact the direction my life takes. I didn't yet realize that God was far more able to help me than I could have ever imagined. But I was captivated by the people, the real, everyday people who shared their stories on the radio programs. I listened with immense curiosity. One mom shared about the devastating loss of her young toddler and how her family had been torn apart by grief. Yet, as she spoke, she conveyed such an amazing sense of hope. Her response to her tragedy made absolutely no sense to me. *How can she be positive in the midst of such suffering?* I wondered. And on another day, a couple shared candidly about how an affair had almost devastated their marriage. Together, leaning on their faith, they shared how their marriage was restored and had become stronger through their adversity. They could have been my next-door neighbors, a coworker, or even me. Both the mom and the couple, in addition to countless other voices on the other side of my car radio, shared about how God gave them the strength and hope they needed to navigate the incredibly difficult challenges in day-to-day life.

At the time, I had no idea that the messages I listened to would become seeds for change, a real change that was closer than I knew. God was slowly helping me shift my focus off of myself and my difficult situation on to Him.

PROTECTED

In life, I have found we don't often choose our flashpoint moments—those moments when, in an instant, change confronts us whether we feel ready for it or not. On a cold winter evening, five and a half years into our marriage, unbeknownst to me, I was about to experience a life-transforming moment. It had been a particularly challenging week because as hard as I continued to try, I couldn't keep Joe happy. I felt my world imploding around me.

I don't remember the specific topic that was the trigger that day, but like any other day, the most unsuspecting topic tripped Joe into an angry tirade. Standing just inches in front of me, rage consumed him as he stared intently at me. In a single swift movement, he raised his fist and drove it into the wall near me. I could feel the impact of Joe's fist throughout my fear-gripped body. He looked long and hard at me and then abruptly turned and walked away. The scene, burned into my memory, played over and over in my mind as though on repeat. *Where did the generous man I married go? How can I possibly gather enough strength to manage my crumbling life?*

Still standing next to the hole in the wall, my mind raced. All the recent radio messages about God that I'd heard on my daily commute welled up and swirled in my mind. Many of those messages reminded me of childhood memories from church and Sunday school, which all seemed so far away now. In that same beautiful church where I had married Joe, I had learned about Bible stories and participated in Christmas pageants that offered hope through inspiring stories. Now, all these years later, strangers on the radio made God sound so close.

Standing in my puddle of fear in our home that day, I wondered, *Where is He? Why does He seem so far away when I need Him so?* I had always believed God was out there, somewhere. But now, filled with fear over Joe's behavior, I felt like God was impossibly far away.

Challenged by those on the radio who told current stories, real people who had found help through their faith in God, I wanted the same for myself and my family. While I didn't know how to reach God, I knew I needed help, and I needed it now.

With a desperate heart and desperate words, standing with my head leaning against the wall, I called out, "God, if You are real—and I think You are—I need You to show up. I need You to show up in a way that I know it is You. I need to know that You are real." My words drifted into the air, leaving me alone in the silence, still desperate.

If life came complete with a soundtrack, the silence that surrounded me in the hallway that night would have been broken just a few days later by a slow and soft but suspenseful melody building in the background. I think of the first *daaaah duuunt* in *Jaws*, when you know the shark is in the water but you haven't seen it yet.

I vividly remember January 9. The day started off like any other workday. The morning, including my twenty-minute commute to the office, was uneventful. But early in the workday, I received a phone call from our au pair. She explained that Ryan, my two-year-old, was covered with hives. I made a quick call to the pediatrician for an appointment and headed home. I felt something stir in me. During the short ride home, the soundtrack I felt within had almost become audible.

When I arrived, I told our nanny that she and my daughter should stay home. For whatever reason, I *knew* they could not come with us. It wasn't up for discussion; the decision was final. I'll be honest. It didn't quite make sense, even to me. On a typical day, if I was out and about, both my son and daughter would join me.

The pediatrician's appointment was unremarkable, though an uneasiness was growing within me. I took Ryan to the car and buckled him into his car seat for our short trip home. When we reached the third traffic light, suddenly I felt very uneasy. This time it was incredibly strong. My heart raced. It made no sense. Still, with every ounce of my being, I felt as though something was about to happen. Something really big.

Sitting at that light, I knew the shortest route home would be to turn right. As I waited for the light to change, the feeling intensified. Before I could decipher what I was feeling and gain control of my racing thoughts, the light changed to green. It may have been the only time in my life that I wanted the light to stay red, at least for a little while longer. For some reason, though it made no sense, I was compelled to go straight. *There, I've decided. Now everything will be fine.* At least that's what I hoped.

A mile down the road, the path I had chosen to take home intersected my original path. Ryan sang cheerfully in his car seat, a welcome distraction to my unsettling feelings. Shortly down the road, his singing abruptly stopped. I wasn't too concerned because it wouldn't have been the first time a car ride had lulled him to sleep. Then the pace of my internal soundtrack quickened. I was on edge. Alert.

Rounding a curve in the road, everything changed. Unbeknownst to me, at the peak of the curve, the roadway was covered in a glassy layer of black ice. In an instant, my van slid out of control. My eyes quickly fixed on the silver SUV coming directly toward us. For one moment, time seemed to stand perfectly still. Never before or since have I felt life shift into what felt like superslow motion, only to be followed by what felt like unbelievable warp speed. No words can ever describe the incredible crash and crunching of metal that followed. After the deafening crunch of our cars colliding came deafening silence. Complete, utter silence. For a moment, I sat still in shock as the airbag deflated with a puff of powder. *I never even saw it inflate*, I thought as I tried to quickly gain my composure.

I reached up and touched my face. It stung from the fresh brush burns from the airbag. I was injured, but okay. Then my thoughts raced to Ryan. *Is he okay?*

Turning in my seat, I looked at my precious two-year-old in the car seat behind me. Remarkably he appeared to be uninjured. He sat contentedly in his seat, quiet. The powder of the deflating airbag lofted in the air, appearing like smoke. Unsure if it was safe to stay in my van, I felt the urge to get us out before a fire or any other resulting danger occurred. Reaching back to Ryan, I somehow *knew* his door wouldn't open. I just knew I needed to take him out through my door. It didn't make sense, but I knew.

We stood by the side of the van and I pulled my cell phone from my purse. Staring at it, I struggled to remember the number to call when there was an emergency. Although the number is so simple, in shock, I couldn't even remember 911.

I dialed my husband instead. "Joe, it's me. We were just in a bad accident," I squeaked out as my tears started to flow. "I know this might sound strange, and I can't explain it, but I think this was supposed to happen." Although I knew it was perhaps the strangest thing to say, I couldn't reconcile the ominous feelings that stirred in me leading up to the accident. At the same time, I struggled to understand the sense of peace, a remarkably soothing, calming, all-consuming peace that washed over me. From the depths of my soul, I knew there was more to the situation, but I definitely didn't understand it and couldn't begin to explain it.

A few minutes later, emergency crews arrived. As the paramedics attended to us, I noticed the damage to the back of my van. "Did the car behind me hit me?" I asked. No, I was told. A witness explained that my van slid on the ice, spinning in a 360-degree circle. We were struck by the SUV on three sides, including Ryan's door, damage I couldn't see from the driver's seat.

My beat-up van sat facing the original direction, totaled by the destruction, part of the engine visibly resting beneath the glove compartment in front of the passenger seat. As I was secured to a backboard and neck brace as a precaution, the paramedics evaluated Ryan. Amazingly, he didn't have a single scratch, bump, or bruise on his body.

Before they finished securing us for transfer to the hospital, a familiar voice shouted out from near the ambulance door: "Is there anything I can do?" It was the friendly voice of Rob, a family friend and neighbor. Rob explained that he'd been a few cars behind us and had recognized my van. He just happened to have his son's car seat in his car and would be happy to take Ryan home if he could be discharged. The coincidence that a trustworthy friend was just behind us and just happened to have a car seat that is *always* in his wife's car didn't go unnoticed. I knew it was more than coincidence. For the first time, I felt as though maybe, just maybe, God had something to do with the events of the day. But it still didn't make any sense.

The ambulance ride to the hospital, while surreal, was also uneventful. After several hours of experiencing such an unshakably ominous feeling, I now felt remarkably at peace.

Later that evening I was released from the hospital with only minor injuries. How we walked away from such a bad accident seemed unexplainable.

The next day, as I rested on the couch nursing my aches, Ryan, full of a two-year-old's energy, bounced around the couch. Suddenly, he said, "Mommy, I saw an angel."

"You did?" I said, shocked.

"It was a boy angel," Ryan continued in his sweet voice.

"When did you see it?" I asked.

"Yesterday." He beamed at me. His eyes grew wide and lit up with excitement as he continued, "It floated outside of the van. Then it was inside the van. He told me everything was going to be okay." Ryan grinned as he recounted his experience.

Goosebumps covered my arms and the hairs on the back of my neck stood up. I looked at Ryan in amazement. I had no idea what to say or how to begin to process what he had just shared. It was then that

I realized that following the accident, Ryan had never cried and hadn't look scared; in fact, he was remarkably peaceful and calm. Now it all made sense. God had been with us, protected us. He certainly had my attention now.

The next Sunday I decided I wanted to attend a local church with the kids. Joe said he didn't care if I went, but wasn't at all interested in coming along. I opened the large white wooden door leading to the sanctuary and slipped into one of the old wooden pews near the back. The light glimmered through the large stained-glass windows along both sides of the church. I took a long, slow, deep breath as I recalled the words I had called out to God just a few days earlier. *I need You to show up.* Sitting there reflecting, I didn't understand it, yet somehow I knew He had.

A few moments later, the congregation stood for the opening hymn. The organist and choir led as everyone joined in singing "Amazing Grace." It was a song I had heard many times as a child. But this time it was different as we sang, "Amazing Grace, how sweet the sound that saved a wretch like me." The words pierced my soul. Tears welled in my eyes and streamed down my cheeks as I struggled to sing along. The words clung to me, washing over my troubled spirit. Through the words of "Amazing Grace," my soul opened to the wonders, mercy, and grace that can come only through Jesus Christ. Within moments, I went from being a broken, hurting wife to being restored. Deep down, I knew my life was forever changed.

In the days following the accident, I worked with our insurance agent to sort out the next steps. We were informed that the police report classified the accident with no fault because of the treacherous road conditions. I was grateful that despite the damage to both vehicles, no one suffered serious physical injury. I felt a sense of relief that the accident could quickly be considered history, without a lasting impact.

My optimism, however, was short-lived. Within days, I received a formal letter that the other driver had acquired the services of an attorney to represent her claim against the insurance company. Fear overcame me as I wondered what the implications would be for me and for us. Not ever having been in a situation like this, I feared being sued and losing everything we had. With the opening of that one envelope, I was introduced to fear in a way I had never known before.

"Joe," I called, "can you read this?" I turned to Joe, hoping he could make sense of the letter. I hoped he could ease my worry.

Instead, the letter instantly ignited Joe's rage. First his expression changed. Then his voice changed. "No one sues us. No one," he fumed as he launched into an intense, profanity-filled, angry tirade. "They won't get away with this. Mark my words. They have no idea who they're dealing with."

In the hours that followed, I listened in horror as Joe called up his "contacts." He plotted that he would send a message to the family and the attorney who sent us the letter. His detailed plans for violence shook me to the core. The minute he got off the phone, I begged him for mercy on their behalf.

Over the next several days I pleaded endlessly for him to let it go. Finally, after several exhausting conversations, he agreed. As long as nothing further came of it, he promised to leave it alone. I desperately prayed for God's intervention. I begged God not to let any of Joe's plans take root. I prayed for complete protection of those to whom Joe wished ill will. And most of all, I prayed for Joe. Who had Joe become? I didn't recognize this stranger.

I was so thankful that nothing more ever came of the letter that had shaken my world. Instead, it served to assist the other driver in her settlement with the insurance company. We never heard anything more.

HOME SWEET HOME?

In the weeks that followed our accident and the letter, Joe displayed a remarkable change. Looking back, I now believe we were temporarily in the "honeymoon" phase of abuse. I didn't see it then. Instead, I was amazed by the transformation I saw before me. At the time, I couldn't help but wonder if Joe realized that in the instant of our car accident he could have lost both Ryan and me. I thought perhaps Joe had experienced an overwhelming shift in perspective because of the accident.

Whatever the source, I treasured the changes I saw within Joe. He became active alongside me in activities with our children once again. Refreshingly, our social group expanded to include a few parents with children the same age as ours. I welcomed this new chapter for our family with excitement. Perhaps I naively hoped that somehow we had moved beyond the issues in our past, though we had done nothing to resolve any of those issues.

On the inside, I clung to my new faith, hoping that somehow it had changed us both. I began attending church on Sundays and I continued to listen to Christian radio on my commute as it provided nourishment for my soul. I began praying for Joe, my children, and our family. I chose to ignore our challenges, much like I had when we'd first dated, earnestly believing we had fully stepped into a new chapter of our family's life. Joe returned convincingly to the Joe I had fallen in love with, so much so that I welcomed his surprise one afternoon a few weeks later.

"I think you and the kids should visit Sweden this summer," he announced.

I looked up, surprised. It hadn't really been anything we had talked about, so the suggestion came out of the blue.

"Jennifer and Ryan are going to continue to suffer the loss of family as each of our au pairs goes home. If we wait until they come back to visit, we have no idea how long they'll have to wait to see them," Joe continued. "And, you haven't been back for years. It would be great for you and your Swedish. And the kids could start to learn Swedish as well."

"Do you really think we could afford it?" I asked, my hopes quickly building.

"I think it's something we just need to do. We'll find a way to make it happen. If I need to cut back in other areas, I will. I'll make it happen," Joe said.

He insisted that we go. In the coming days, we booked the trip for the kids and me. Joe declined to join us saying that he had no interest in traveling in a country where he could not understand what was being said around him. It had been several years since I had been back to Sweden so I was thrilled at the opportunity. I planned a marvelous two-week trip visiting old friends as well as our recent au pairs, including Sarah.

During our exciting two-week adventure, we drove from Stockholm to Gothenburg visiting friends and taking in spectacular sites. It truly was a dream vacation from start to finish. From giant Viking stones, beautiful historic castles, quaint towns and beautiful lakes, the trip provided a well-needed escape. Our kid-friendly itinerary included stops such as a candy shop where we watched giant peppermint sticks being made, the candy pulled between large paddles much the same as the way saltwater taffy is made. Nearby, we were captivated as a glass blower pulled an orange glowing mass out of a stone oven.

"What's he making?" Ryan asked, his eyes as wide as saucers.

"I don't know. We'll have to keep watching," I said as the man continued to work swiftly, pulling and tapping.

"It's an elephant," I said joking, not yet seeing what the figurine would be, but knowing it definitely wasn't an elephant.

"No, it isn't," Jennifer said. Both kids grew silent, mesmerized by the glass object taking shape before us. The man made a few final swift movements and then with his large gloved hand picked up the piece and set it on a table near the viewing area where we stood.

"It's a dog!" the kids said unanimously, excited to see something recognizable from what moments before had been an unidentifiable glowing mass.

In addition to the incredible sites, we enjoyed visits with our extended family, our previous au pairs. Among our visits was a stop at Sarah's parents' house where they hosted us for several days on their country farm. Their farm seemed worlds away from the hustle and bustle of Stockholm, which capped off our amazing trip. The two weeks melted away and it was soon time to return to our regular routines and everyday life.

During the spring following our trip to Sweden, Joe and I decided to buy our first single-family home. It was a dream come true. We spent many afternoons driving around neighborhoods looking for one we could call our own. Oh, how easy it was to fall in love with several houses in the new developments popping up in our Washington, DC, suburb. It didn't take long before we realized that once you added in the amenities that made the model homes so beautiful, the price wasn't anywhere near what the "starting at" signs advertised, which was all we could afford. A balance of regular reality checks and persistence paid off when we found one that was just right. Sure it needed some fixing up, but we saw past the foil wallpaper in the living room, the avocado appliances, and the deep, rust-colored shag carpet in the family room. We knew that with a bit of work and a little love, this three-bedroom split-level could be transformed into our home.

Once the sellers accepted our offer on the house, settlement day came quickly. After surviving the seemingly endless process of signing and initialing a large stack of papers, we signed our names one last time and the keys were ours. We spent the rest of the day unloading the overstuffed U-Haul in the driveway before running out of time and energy. Exhausted, we collapsed into bed, proud new homeowners.

Our new suburb could have passed for Mayberry. Our small Maryland town didn't have so much as one traffic light. Instead, the center of town was marked by a simple four-way stop. There were two community parks in town, one just at the end of our street. On any typical weekend, the neighborhood buzzed with activity—children rode bikes, dads played ball with their children, families walked. Here, neighbors knew one another. This seemed to be the perfect place to raise our children.

The next day, a knock at the door brought the first delivery to our new home. A man stood on our porch holding a large plant. It was a gorgeous ceramic pot bursting with a variety of large beautiful plants, with a card tucked in the brilliant green leaves. I knew in an instant it was from my parents. My mother's passion for gardening was often visible in her gifts. This was perhaps the largest indoor plant I had ever seen, a hallmark of my mother's touch. I pulled the card out and read, "Congratulations on your new home. Love, Mom and Dad/Nana and Poppop." I smiled, appreciating the thoughtfulness and sentiment behind their beautiful gift.

Initially, Joe said nothing about the plant or the note. Instead, he was noticeably silent. It wasn't until much later that night that Joe erupted in anger.

"I can't believe they would do that," Joe said.

"Do what?" I innocently asked, having no idea why he sounded so angry.

"Did you read the card?" Joe asked, his words sharp and full of emotion. He snatched the card from the planter with a swift motion and thrust it toward me.

I took the card, glancing at it again. It was unassuming, a typical card that might come with any floral arrangement, barely big enough for the message scrawled on it. My eyes scanned the card, rereading it. "Congratulations on your new home. Love, Mom and Dad/Nana and Poppop." Laying the card next to the planter, I said, "Yes, I read it. Why?" I still didn't see anything unusual that could cause him to be so upset.

"How is it signed?" he fumed.

"Love, Mom and Dad/Nana and Poppop."

"Exactly!" Joe said. "The plant and the congratulations aren't for us as a couple or us as a family. It's for you and the kids."

"What are you talking about?" I asked Joe, truly puzzled.

"How do they usually sign cards for me?"

"With their names and as mom and dad," I answered.

"They didn't sign their names. They only signed Mom and Dad/Nana and Poppop. They didn't intend for it to be for me too."

"Joe, it's a small card. There isn't space to write anything else on it," I said picking the card up to show him.

"I know what it looks like," Joe snapped. "They did this deliberately."

Offended that my parents did not sign their first names, Joe was convinced they were congratulating me and our children, not him or us as a family. He fumed that on this wonderful occasion of our purchasing our first single-family home, he had been horribly disrespected.

"Why else would they have excluded me?" Joe demanded.

"Joe, there was no more room on the card. I know my parents and it is clearly for us," I tried to explain. But, no matter how hard I tried to convince him, his anger only deepened. In the end, I retreated upstairs, stunned and confused that a gift could fuel so much anger.

That night was cool for April, both inside and outside. Despite the coming spring, the temperatures had become quite frigid. The next morning, I slid open the curtains to our patio. Frost glistened on the blades of grass in the morning light. Soaking in the view, knowing this was now our yard, I took it all in. Happy. At peace. Then something on the patio caught my eye.

There, next to our outdoor furniture, was the plant we had received from my parents. Thick frost glistened in the morning light on the plant's wilted and drooping leaves. After I had gone to bed, Joe had purposefully put the plant outside, knowing the cold night would likely kill it. It did.

We never talked about the plant after that day. Deep down, I think I knew at that point that we had more issues than a dead plant. Not knowing how to deal with any of it, I buried my sadness and instead focused on the positive. Our focus together became the house and our children. We dove into remodeling our home; we picked out a nice blue pile carpet to replace the rust shag after we painted the dark wood paneling a bright white. Then we tore down the dated wallpaper in the kitchen and replaced it with a fresh coat of paint trimmed with a sunny boarder.

Within a few weeks, the cold weather finally gave way to beautiful spring weather. Joe and I agreed that one of our first additions to our new home needed to be a swing set to adorn our new fenced yard. After searching several stores, we found one guaranteed to fill our backyard with endless giggles and squeals of delight. It came complete with a slide, two swings, a monkey bar, and a teeter-totter. However, there was one catch. It required assembly. To be honest, we were completely unprepared for the vast amount of assembly required. As we unfolded the instructions, one fold after the next, the paper quickly multiplied in size, giving way to an extremely large instruction sheet. The complexity of the diagrams before us should have served as a warning. For all of the "some assembly required" projects we had tackled together, that swing set still to this day holds the distinct honor of being the most complicated project we ever tackled. Truth be told, we didn't even complete it ourselves. When our patience failed before the pile of parts resembled a swing set, Joe called his cousin to come rescue us.

Enticed by the warmer weather, I also learned to rollerblade. Our neighborhood proved to be a wonderful place to head out with Jennifer and Ryan in our double jog stroller while I pushed them and glided along behind them. I poured myself into my role as mother, finding solace in the time I spent with my children. At times, Joe joined in and we laughed and chatted as we played outside or took walks through the neighborhood, basking in the warmth of being together. Everyone loved Joe. He was warm and charming. Those are memories I still cherish. I still have adorable pictures of Joe giving piggyback rides to our children as we navigated the panda exhibit or the monkey house on trips to the zoo. But as sweet as many of those memories are, during that same time, Joe's alter ego began to develop in earnest.

While from the outside our family appeared idyllic, behind closed doors we were struggling. Joe seemed to feel threatened by people in my life, so isolating me seemed to be a subconscious win-win. Spending time with friends, even female friends, brought endless scrutiny from him. I found out later that at the same time Joe had also begun controlling my contact with people outside of our home. Countless times when my family called, Joe would answer and tell them, "I'm sorry, she's busy with the children. I'll let her know you called." It wasn't until years later that my mother told me about the many, many missed calls and messages. She assumed I knew, so she never thought to tell me. She figured I was too busy with two kids to call her back, so we talked whenever I called her or answered the phone when she called. With fewer people close to me, keeping up the ruse that everything was okay became significantly easier. At the same time, it reduced Joe's need to question my loyalty. I really don't think it was a conscious decision on my part but rather the path of least resistance that naturally evolved as I tried to keep the peace at any cost.

Life just wasn't getting any easier. Joe began drinking daily. His beer consumption increased with time and turned into day-long binges that began shortly after breakfast. His habits and patterns slowly began to change. He stopped joining our au pair, the kids, and me for dinner and, instead, listened to music with his oversized headphones or stood on our porch, a cigarette in one hand, a beer in the other. He developed a new habit of leaving half-consumed beer cans in his wake. Many became portable ashtrays giving off the distinct aroma of an old bar room—the unpleasant combination of stale beer and cigarette smoke.

When I asked him about the increase, he denied that he drank much at all, citing the half-empty cans as evidence that he wasn't consuming as much as it might appear. In my heart, I hoped I had exaggerated the increase. Instead, I realized that beer breathed life into a different side of Joe. The more he drank, the more we fought. The more we fought, the more I saw a very dark and angry Joe.

His words transformed into knives, regularly tearing through me, leaving gaping wounds—though none of them visible: "You're useless." "You're a pathetic mother." "No one could ever love you." "I made you who you are. Without me, you'd be nothing."

The sources of our conflicts were many. If we had fought about only one thing, perhaps the outbursts could have been more predictable. Instead, anything could anger him in an instant and would erupt into full and intense conflicts. I tried to learn from past conflicts in hopes of learning how to avoid new ones. But that never worked.

Nothing I did or didn't do could influence Joe's outbursts. He was becoming ever more volatile.

We fought about finances, about housekeeping, and about how to raise our children. While Joe had strong opinions on each of those topics, he rarely did anything to help manage any of them. The issues, from his perspective, were entirely my fault.

While the outbursts were intense, painful, numbing, there was another side to life with Joe. After an argument, life would become wonderful again. Joe would return to the generous, suave, kind man I'd married. He would shower me with compliments, gifts, and affection.

In the beginning, his outbursts came months apart, almost far enough apart for me to have hoped that a permanent change had occurred. Life became peaceful, wonderfully peaceful. I'd bask in our picture-perfect family—vacations to the beach, holding hands with a sweet Joe while we took long walks with our children in their stroller on the boardwalk. Those wonderful memories are forever etched in my mind.

Ironically, it was some of these later vacations that brought to light just how much alcohol Joe was consuming. On one trip, I had planned a getaway for us to a cabin in the Pennsylvania mountains. We had been to this beautiful lakeside retreat many times before, and it had become one of our favorite places. There we enjoyed swimming, hiking, kayaking, and just getting away. This time, as we loaded our minivan, carefully placing our luggage, the kids' toys, and everything we'd need for our short getaway, Joe tucked four cubes of beer into the lot. Knowing we'd be gone for just five days, I was shocked by how much beer he'd packed for just himself. Each cube contained thirty beers, so it was hard for me to deny it any longer: Joe was addicted.

Somewhere in the early years of our marriage, beer had become an integral part of Joe's life. It wasn't the beer itself that I learned to hate but the person Joe became when he consumed it. It made no difference how beautiful we made our home or how successful our careers were; a gray cloud loomed over us. I desperately wanted to keep the peace in our home. I thought, *If only I try harder, if only I keep the house clean, the bills paid, and Joe happy, maybe it will be better.* But nothing was ever enough.

SEEING THE LIGHT

Over the coming months, the challenges with Joe propelled me to begin seeking out God in earnest. I found that the more I leaned on Him, the more I could see my own situation clearly. It was as though I had been living in total darkness. The more I prayed, read the Bible, and listened to that Christian radio station, the more light was shined into my world. Stories on the radio that once seemed so foreign began to resonate with me, feeding my famished soul. The hope that I had heard in the stories when I first began listening began to feel like hope not just for them but for me too. I remember one woman sharing so transparently about the challenges she faced after losing her husband suddenly. Despite the tragedy, she didn't sound devastated, but rather confidently conveyed joy, hope, and peace through her story. Listening reassured me that I too could gain clarity and hope.

With fresh eyes I began to see more clearly the obstacles in my daily life. I began realizing just how manipulative and controlling Joe had become. His own unwarranted insecurities regularly fueled his paranoia. Anything, even a long-running Sunday church service, could trigger Joe's anger.

One Sunday, a baptism caused our church service to run longer than normal. In addition, the kids and I lingered in fellowship after the service, tempted by the trays full of appetizers and desserts. A baptism and fellowship can add quite a bit of time to a typical Sunday service. I didn't give it a second thought. Joe usually didn't mind if I took our children to church, though he never joined us himself.

But that particular Sunday, when we arrived home, Joe was furious. "Where have you been?" he lashed out.

"At church," I responded.

"It never runs this long. Where were you?"

"Joe, I was at church. There was a baptism today. It ran long."

He looked at me with eyes that could pierce steel. "Who is he?" He paused. With greater accusation, he pressed again. "I said who is he?" His intense stare paralyzed me.

Before I could answer, he snarled, "Oh, never mind, you're useless." With one swift motion he slipped on his oversized headphones, grabbed a beer, and pressed play. The conversation was over. I had been dismissed. Joe escaped to his music and beer, something he did often. When he did, it was as though he disappeared. He may have been physically present, but in reality, he was absent—disconnected from us.

During the summer that followed, we welcomed our new au pair Sofia. Her bright, sunny disposition shone through with her first hello. She had a distinctly Swedish accent when she spoke, although her long, wavy, red hair and freckles didn't fit the stereotypical image of a young Swede. I hoped and prayed that Joe would get along with her, knowing if the two of them couldn't get along, the challenges in my life would multiply.

Soon after Sofia arrived, Joe invited her to step out onto the porch while he had a cigarette. In the past, Joe often called our au pairs out onto the porch to "talk" while he smoked. The porch was his stage, home of his soapbox. Typically when he invited someone out to the porch, it meant he had a monologue he felt compelled to deliver and required an audience. Typically when Joe said, "Step outside with me for a moment," the firmness in his voice dispelled any opposition. For the most part, I think our au pairs listened with one ear, always taking what he said with a grain of salt. Sofia was different. She arrived to our home with excitement in her eyes, ready for the world of possibilities in the year ahead.

She immediately hit it off with the kids and me. And while her first impression of Joe might also have been positive, that quickly changed once Joe invited her out to the porch. I knew he wanted to talk to her about his expectations and ensure that she was on the same page with regard to caring for our children. When they came back inside from their talk, everything seemed fine. She spent time playing with Jennifer and Ryan and talking to us to get to know us better. Later Joe ran an errand and invited Sofia along so that she could see a little bit of our town. Everything was exactly how I would expect; the day seemed textbook for every other day we had welcomed a new au pair. I couldn't have been more wrong. At some point in the evening, Sofia emerged from her room. Her bright disposition had completely washed away, almost as though she had seen a ghost. "My mom would like to talk to you," she said softly, handing me the phone.

"Hello, this is Susan."

"Sofia would like to come home. Is she okay? Is she safe?" her mother asked.

"Yes, she's safe," I answered, startled by the questions.

"She has contacted the agency. They will pick her up in the morning if she is okay to stay until then."

"Yes, of course that's okay," I said.

"Thank you," her mother said as we hung up the phone.

What had happened? Something had gone horribly wrong in the few hours Sofia was at our home. But what? A million questions swirled through my mind, though I had no answers. Sofia became completely withdrawn. She wasn't willing to talk about what had changed or what had happened. How had everything gone from what appeared to be perfect one minute to Sofia's fleeing the next? The only thing that was abundantly clear was that Sofia wanted out as fast as possible. Although I had absolutely no idea what had transpired, I was certain of one thing: It had to do with Joe.

CROSSING THE LINE

After Sofia left, the au pair agency quickly placed Anna in our home, which allowed life to continue without missing a beat. When she arrived, Joe took a far more passive role, allowing me to work with her as she got to know our children and adjusted to our home and routines. Over time, Joe continued to use music and beer to escape, while I found my own new escape by way of my faith. I discovered that listening to Christian music as well as praying regularly provided me the encouragement and hope to survive day to day. During this same time, my friend and coworker Cherie also found herself hungry for God, which led us to spend some of our lunch breaks in prayer at a nearby church. Fairly new to my faith, I was often unsure what to read in the Bible, what to pray for, or how to pray. My prayers were simple, though I admit a bit repetitive. Every day I had the same simple request: *Lord, please help Joe learn who You are. Please give me strength and wisdom in my relationship with Joe. Please be present in our lives. And, Lord, please help me be a better mom.*

One day, I decided to break this pattern of prayer. Instead, I wanted to spend the time reading the Bible and reflecting. Not having any idea where to begin, I decided to let my Bible fall open and read the passage it opened to. As the pages fell open, I looked down and began reading Psalm 144:1–2.

> "Praise be to the Lord my Rock,
> who trains my hands for war,
> my fingers for battle.
> He is my loving God and my fortress,
> my stronghold and my deliverer,
> my shield, in whom I take refuge."

My eyes skipped down the page and I continued reading:

> "Part your heavens, Lord, and come down;
> touch the mountains, so that they smoke.
> Send forth lightning and scatter the enemy;
> shoot your arrows and rout them.
> Reach down your hand from on high;
> deliver me and rescue me
> from the mighty waters,
> from the hands of foreigners
> whose mouths are full of lies,
> whose right hands are deceitful." (Psalm 144:5–8)

Who trains my hands for war? I thought. *I'm not at war.* I closed my Bible and flipped the pages. I let it fall open again. I looked down. *Interesting*, I thought. Once again, my Bible had opened to Psalm 144. I read the passage a second time, reading it more slowly and reflectively. With my eyes closed, I flipped through the pages of my Bible a third time. I opened my eyes as the pages fell open to Psalm 144 for a third time! Convinced my Bible must have a crease in the pages, or the binding, or some other logical explanation, I picked up a pew Bible. I said *God, please show me whatever it is You want me to read and ponder.*

I let the pew Bible fall open. Leaning forward, I looked down as my eyes focused on the page.

> "Praise be to the Lord my Rock,
> who trains my hands for war,
> my fingers for battle." (Psalm 144:1)

Over the coming days, I revisited this psalm many, many times, seeking to understand the words that seemed to haunt me.

It wouldn't be long before I realized, through the words of Psalm 144, what God was preparing me for.

One afternoon that December, my life went from bad to worse in a matter of minutes. I was in the kitchen cleaning up when Joe walked in. "We need to talk," he said.

There's something about those four words that so easily and instantly conjure anxiety, especially when accompanied by Joe's icy tone. This time was no different. I stopped what I was doing and turned to look at Joe.

"You know that Sarah's coming to visit for three weeks," he started.

It had been two years since Sarah had lived with us, but still we kept in touch. She was one of those people in your life who isn't related to you but over time becomes family. Now home in Sweden, she planned to visit us. She was still like a sister to me, and an aunt to my children. We were all looking forward to her visit.

"Before she comes," he continued, "I need to tell you something." He paused and shifted his focus to the floor in front of his feet. His voice cracked as he continued, "There's no easy way to say this so I'm going to just blurt it out. She and I are in a relationship." His voice trailed off as he spoke. Clearing his throat, he continued, "We have been for over two years. I'm only telling you because her mother found out. She said if I don't tell you, she will. She thought you should know."

The words instantly cut like a knife through my heart as a million thoughts raced through my head. But before I had the chance to formulate a response, Joe went on the offensive. "She's still coming," he continued quickly, "and she'll stay in our house. You *will* be nice to her."

What?! I screamed in my head.

Joe's disposition changed, and his eyes became cold and stony. He moved directly in front of me and continued, "You don't have a choice."

With every ounce of me, I spat out, "Yes, I do," my mind still racing.

He abruptly responded, "No, you don't. She's coming."

"Then I'll leave."

"Oh, you can leave. But you can't take the kids." I stood frozen in shock and disbelief as Joe continued. "You know no one will raise my kids but me." He paused, letting his words settle. "Do you know who you're dealing with?"

A chill went down my spine. If it is possible to peer directly into the eyes of pure evil, standing in my kitchen on that mid-December day, I experienced the chilling, awful experience of just that. It was not a feeling I had ever felt before, nor have I since.

Joe continued, calmly and coldly. He explained what would happen if I ever tried to leave him. "Make no mistake, I will kill you, and

I won't get caught for it. Do you know who you're dealing with?" he repeated. With great precision, every detail accounted for, he outlined his chilling plan. Not only did his plan detail how he would kill me, it outlined his impeccable alibi. He had thought of everything. "You won't get away from me. If you run, I will find you." It was obvious this wasn't the first time he had given his plan consideration.

Joe continued, saying that if I ran, he would kill my parents. Knowing I am close to them, he bragged, "When you come back for their funerals, I'll get you. Don't ever underestimate me, and don't ever forget who you are dealing with, ever."

I was numb, too numb to even form tears. I was paralyzed by an intense fear that overcame my entire being. Standing there, not knowing what to say or do, I prayed for strength. Instantly, from the depths of my being, words began to rise. "Praise be to the Lord my Rock, who trains my hands for war, my fingers for battle. He is my loving God and my fortress, my stronghold and my deliverer, my shield, in whom I take refuge" (Psalm 144:1–2). Psalm 144 swelled in my heart: *My loving God and fortress, my stronghold and my deliverer.* Suddenly I knew God already knew right where I was. Not only did He know, but when Psalm 144 kept "finding" me, He knew how much I would need those words.

For eight years, I'd hoped my marriage could endure the disagreements, my husband's drinking, and the overwhelming challenges we faced. For years, I hid in denial of how bad it had become. But for all the issues I denied or overlooked, another woman in the middle of my marriage was more than I could ignore. Despite Joe's reluctant confession and chilling words, I wanted my marriage restored. My vows were not something I took lightly. While I had no idea how it would be possible, I wanted to put the pieces of our marriage back together. I wasn't ready to throw in the towel and walk away. Searching for an answer, I asked Joe if he would consider going to marriage counseling with me. I thought maybe someone who helped others for a living could help us sort out this mess. But without hesitation, Joe abruptly told me no.

I knew we couldn't fix this on our own, though counseling wasn't anything I'd ever contemplated. To salvage our marriage, I was willing to try. I wanted the kind, generous, suave Joe all the time. I had seen that Joe often. Where was he now? Couldn't we change? Couldn't he change?

Instead, Joe argued that counseling would only put someone else in the middle of our problems. "What happens in our home is the business of our home alone," he said. He was adamant; he would absolutely never consider a marriage counselor.

The rest of that weekend remains a blur. I was consumed by despair and swallowed up by my brokenness. Numb and barely functioning, I took care of our children as though I were on autopilot. I avoided Joe, hoping to avoid the reality of my situation. The next clear memory I have is returning to work that Monday morning, desperately wanting to stay alone in that elevator. But, I knew I needed to face the day ahead. I hoped to slip into my office unnoticed. Instead I walked directly into the path of an enthusiastic coworker, with a cheery greeting, "Did you have a good weekend?" She had no idea about the devastation that tore through my world since Friday afternoon. My forced "*Mm-hmm. Have a great day,*" spared me from the truth.

My heart sank as I realized my true response, *No, actually, my weekend was awful. My husband confessed to an affair with a family friend and vowed to kill me if I made any attempt to leave. I truly believe he would because I know it's something he is completely capable of.*

In the week that followed, I struggled to make sense of all this on my own. I knew that on my own I couldn't untangle the mess my life had become; I needed help. I decided to seek out a Christian counselor. As much as I wanted help and support, I wanted someone who could understand my newfound faith. Conflicted, I really didn't want to pursue a divorce, but I had no idea what my next step should be. Honestly, I didn't know if counseling could even help my situation. I didn't think I needed to change; Joe did. And, if Joe could change, we'd be fine. Right? Still, I thought it might be worth a try.

Through a local Christian counseling group I found Molly, a counselor who would soon become a valued resource. She was able to work my appointments into my lunch break during work, making it easy to slip away unnoticed by Joe and eliminating the potential questions or scrutiny I would have received from him. It was surprising how easy it was to talk to her. I had become so accustomed to holding on to the details of my life as secrets that I locked away. During my first session, I found it easy to share the simple facts. Our conversation started with my family background, my age, what I did for a living, my marriage of eight years, and that I had two beautiful children. What had brought me to counseling? Even my answer to that question seemed easy to share, because although we had many problems, an affair was something I had heard of before. The other problems, such as the alcoholism and abuse, were problems I still struggled to understand. Foreign to me, those issues would take longer to share.

As I continued sharing the details of my life with Molly, I began to see the picture of my life in a whole new light. I realized how absurd my situation had become. Revealing more of the pieces of my story to Molly would take time. Before I could really open up, I needed to develop trust in her. There were countless details of my life that I had shared with no one. Not even my closest friends or family had any idea of the private hell my life had become. Looking back, I know Molly knew that there was much more long before I was willing to share. But she allowed me to share at my own pace. I found working with her a bit like solving a puzzle. I thought I knew what most of the pieces looked like, though with time, I realized it was helpful to take out the pieces one at a time, turn each one over, and try to understand where or how it connected to the rest of the puzzle. In life, we don't have the luxury of looking at the puzzle's box top for quick answers. Instead, I started to turn to God and trust Him for an understanding of the pieces of my life. Prayer and journaling became key to helping me do just that. While I was fearful that Joe might find my journals, I found that writing out my prayers and thoughts helped tremendously. To ensure my safety, I took the precaution to not just hide my journals, but to also write in Swedish. Additionally, I read books like Max Lucado's *Just Like Jesus*, which offered me tremendous hope. It would take me months to realize that I had slowly lost my voice over eight years of marriage. My life choices were driven more out of fear than out of hope or love. Years of Joe's reminders of how useless I was had taken a toll on me.

The voices on the radio station during my commute continued to convey hope, which I hungered for. One morning during my commute, my thoughts were interrupted by an advertisement for a *Family Life Today* call-in segment. I couldn't imagine calling in to a program; but the two hosts, Dennis Rainey and Bob Lepine, sounded so caring and grounded. Their daily broadcast seemed to effectively equip families, which gave me hope that just maybe they might have some words of wisdom that could help me. I jotted down the number and time of the segment while considering if I could work up the courage to call. Later that afternoon, I slipped into a conference room at work. Still fairly new to exploring my own faith, I welcomed the opportunity to hear from two men with more mature faith. I glanced down at the number scrawled on the paper in my hand. *This is crazy*, I thought. My heart began to race. *Should I really call?* With a gulp, I nervously dialed, unsure how I really expected two strangers on the other end of a phone line to help. Still, I hoped for a dose of inspired wisdom that would offer me the strength I so desperately needed.

I don't remember the specific details of my conversation all those years ago. What I do still remember today is how surprised I was by the compassion of the two hosts. No, I didn't provide all of the specifics; I did paint enough of the picture for them to understand that my life had been turned upside down by an unfaithful husband. They couldn't fix the mess my life had become with just a brief conversation, but their listening brought comfort to my broken heart. They agreed that it would be inappropriate for Sarah to stay in our home and understood my heartbreak. Before we hung up, they asked if they could pray for me. "Yes," I said. As they prayed, an unexplainable peace washed over me. With an "amen" and a "God bless you," the conversation ended. Somehow even though life wasn't magically better, I felt in that moment that God heard my plight. And although our paths crossed for only a few moments, I felt God's love through the voices of those two strangers on the phone who were over a thousand miles away.

The wisdom of the radio hosts underscored what I knew in my head but felt powerless to implement. I knew Joe needed an ultimatum. I knew what he was doing was unacceptable. But knowing it and feeling empowered to fix the mess I was in were two entirely different things. In order to build my strength, I continued attending counseling with Molly. She recommended I read the book *Boundaries: When to Say YES, How to Say NO to Take Control of Your Life* by Dr. Henry Cloud and Dr. John Townsend. The title sounded intriguing. Over the coming weeks I devoured every word, hoping for insight that could bring relief to my nightmarish world. The book helped me understand that establishing my own boundaries in life could help me disengage from Joe's manipulative ways. I intensely studied the chapters that discussed mental, physical, emotional, and spiritual boundaries and found valuable, actionable advice. The insight the book provided allowed me to see how Joe's emotional abuse over the years had robbed me of any healthy boundaries between us. His devastating actions stole my voice. He had limited my actions while manipulating my emotions. In realizing that I was not the first person to struggle with boundaries, I gained one of the most powerful insights that I could. I felt new hope in knowing that others had overcome the challenges of implementing appropriate personal boundaries resulting in a healthier life.

Although I didn't yet feel as though I could unilaterally implement boundaries in all aspects of my relationship with Joe, I began asserting myself more as I began to establish new boundaries. One simple step I took was that I stopped buying Joe beer. Although he would often ask me to stop to pick it up for him, I conveniently forgot to stop. I knew it would be better to tell Joe no, but while I worked up the courage to say no with my voice, I began saying no with my actions. It was one small step in the right direction and one small step that I took to stop enabling him. It was a boundary that I knew I needed. Eventually he stopped asking me to buy him beer because he knew I wouldn't bring it home. Without question, it was a pivotal moment; I had begun the search for my lost voice.

DELIVER ME!

As I embraced the idea of boundaries, a situation came up where I welcomed the opportunity to assert myself. While having lunch at work one day, Cherie and I discovered that we both wanted to see a new movie that had just been released. That December, after many months of trailers, the story of Moses came to the big screen in the *Prince of Egypt*. Popular songs such as "When You Believe," written by Stephen Schwartz and sung by Mariah Carey and Whitney Houston, received much radio airtime. The hype leading up to the movie made it one I did not want to miss. While Joe wasn't thrilled that I had Saturday plans, he said he didn't mind as long as our au pair would be home and could watch our children.

I hoped the movie might be a wonderful escape from the chaos in my life, a desperately needed respite. The movie opened to a dramatic scene with the song "Deliver Us," also written by Schwartz. Slaves in the Egyptian desert struggled to build monuments for Pharaoh. The powerful music and dramatic cinematography came to life, drawing me in as the Hebrews cried out to God for help. They were not free to live as they chose, nor could they leave. Instead, they were governed by Pharaoh's heavy, oppressive fist. Sitting in the theater, their desperate plight came alive for me.

Though I was not a slave, I suddenly realized that I was living in bondage. My freedom had been stolen by my husband. With their cry, "Deliver us!" I was drawn into the movie. No longer looking for respite, I found myself soul searching, looking for hope. For the next hour and a half I was transported to a place far away. As though I had traveled through time and space, my heart broke, feeling the pain and struggle of the Hebrews. Hearing their cry to God, I longed for their freedom. After seeing their immense struggle and God's faithfulness to deliver them, I was left in awe of the power of God.

Let my people go, echoed in my mind as I left the theater. It resonated as though I were looking back at the world from far away with God's perspective. Thoughts raced through my mind. *I am not free. Instead, I'm imprisoned by Joe. And, though I don't know them, there are countless others who also aren't free. Stuck in either a self-made prison or one made by others, they are prevented from living the life God intends.* And then, as though hearing God's heart, *Let my people go!* echoed again in my mind. An ache swelled, filling my body, even my bones, as if God were allowing me to experience, in a small way, his ache for His children like me. I began to realize that excuses are so easy to come by and may sometimes seem easier than pressing into God to see what His will is rather than our own. I'm sure Moses might have preferred that God had picked someone else. Instead, he was faithful, which in turn brought freedom to the Hebrews.

Heading home to the very situation that entrapped me, my heart continued aching—for me and for others. I longed for Moses-like courage to follow God despite all difficulties and obstacles. Thankful for having witnessed the Bible come to life through the magic of animation, I had no idea how my own journey would unfold. Equipped with a new soundtrack, my heart found peace in that reminder of God's faithfulness all those years ago.

That would prove powerful in the months to come.

The next day Joe, Jennifer, Ryan, and I headed to the outskirts of our small town to a Christmas tree farm. Together, we trekked up and down the rows of evergreens searching for the perfect Christmas tree, just like we had done so many years prior. That year though, the process of finding our tree seemed so empty and hollow. I pooled all of my energy to remain outwardly excited by our expedition. Seeing the enthusiasm in my children's faces gave me the inspiration needed to help with the search.

"What about this one?" Jennifer asked tugging the branch of a large tree.

"Over here! What about this one?" Ryan chimed in, pointing at an oversized tree a few rows over.

But neither of those trees was big enough for Joe. Instead, he liked to find the tallest, fullest tree that we could find that would be just about too big for our living room. Not until we found *that* tree could we call it our own. After each of the kids suggested several trees, we turned and walked down to the end of a row. There it stood tall and proud. We all knew that was *the* tree. A few minutes later, the Christmas tree farmer helped us cut down the tree. He helped us mount it on top of my van for the short ride home.

Once home we sipped hot chocolate with whipped cream to the heartwarming sounds of Christmas music. Drinking in the moment,

I felt as if our life was almost normal. Christmas almost felt intact. Together, we decorated our tree with the ornaments we had collected as a family. On Christmas Eve night, Joe helped me stuff the stockings and wrap the presents as though nothing had changed.

Christmas that year cast a gloomy shadow in my heart, but no one was the wiser. Our tree was lit with both colorful and white Christmas lights. The ornaments had been placed on the tree with care. Under the tree, festive presents were decorated with bows while stockings were stuffed, hanging from the fireplace.

The sweet giggles of my children broke the morning air. It was Christmas.

Since finding my faith anew, I had found a beautifully illustrated children's book of the Christmas story. A few Christmases earlier, I had suggested to Joe that we adopt reading it as a new family tradition. He welcomed the idea of an established tradition, given that his own family life had been so fractured when he was growing up. I treasured the tradition as a way to help us remember the true meaning of Christmas. This year, once again, we sat together and read the Christmas story before the first piece of wrapping paper was torn. Then, like on so many other Christmases, the room was filled with the sounds of Christmas songs on the radio, paper tearing, boxes ripping, and children squealing. The best gift I gave my children that year? The joy of celebrating a child's innocent Christmas without the knowledge of their mother's internal pain.

Christmas Day too quickly came and went that year, and with its passing, my most dreaded day—December 26—dawned. Sarah's arrival day. Still consumed with my internal struggle, every fiber of my being screaming *no*, I amassed all of my strength and energy to face the day. To my children however, it was an exciting day. Over the years, Sarah had become an extension of our family. They hadn't seen her in some time, so their excitement was genuine. For me, her arrival was quite different. It was perhaps one of the most surreal moments of my life. A woman who had become like family to me, now the lover of my husband and friend to my children, entered my home and wished me a "Merry Christmas."

Looking back, I have to admit, much of Sarah's visit is a jumbled mess of memories. I lived moment to moment, numb, simply existing. It didn't take long before Sarah confronted me; in fact, it was only the second day of her visit. We both knew there was an elephant in the room. She was the first with a desire to talk about it. As I washed up dishes in the sink, Sarah came in and interrupted me.

"Just so you know," she started, "I will never leave him."

I looked up at her, making eye contact. "I plan to fight for my marriage," I responded.

"I won't give up. Even if I have to stay the other woman forever, I will." I was floored. What woman sets out to be and stay the "other woman"? Standing in the kitchen of my home, with the giggles of my children spilling in from the next room, she pledged her unwavering love for Joe. She wanted me to know that she wasn't going anywhere. I was amazed by her audacity.

To say New Year's Eve was a unique holiday that year would be a laughable understatement. Sure, it had all the typical trimmings of shrimp cocktail, cheese and crackers, noisemakers, hats, and a TV broadcast of the ball drop in New York. But unlike other holidays, mine came complete with betrayal, infidelity, abuse, and a broken heart. *Happy New Year*, I thought.

Since New Year's Day fell on a Friday, Joe and I both were off work until Monday. Under normal circumstances, the extra time might have been relaxing. It's usually lovely when the weekend falls after a holiday. This year, my time off was anything but restful. Sunday night, my mind struggled to return to routine and "work" mode. Jennifer and Ryan already in bed, I started up the stairs. "Good night," I called out insincerely to Joe and Sarah sitting on the couch in our living room.

As I reached the top of the stairs, I heard Joe call, "Susan." Tempted to ignore him or pretend I hadn't heard him, I turned to find him at the bottom of the stairs peering up at me. "If I fall asleep down here, can you make sure I'm up in the morning?" he asked.

With that one question, Joe took his defiance to a new level. It was not enough that he was having an affair. It was not enough that his affair was with a close friend or that he brought her into our home. He now planned to spend the night on the couch with her, while I, his wife, and his children slept upstairs.

Appalled, I gathered strength to pull out a whisper: "Sure." Though my voice said yes, my tone and body language said absolutely, positively no! In my heart and in my mind, I knew without reservation that there was no way I would wake him the next morning if he didn't find his way upstairs on his own. It was one small step in setting a boundary that I felt safe setting.

I dreaded returning to work. I knew Monday's return to work would be peppered with "Happy New Year!" "How was your vacation?" "Was Santa good to you?" and "Did you do anything fun?" Without a good response, I simply wanted the merriment and Sarah's stay to be past once and for all.

Her visit extended two weeks into the New Year. Daily, I painted on a contented face so others could not see my internal pain. The two long weeks required significant energy to keep up the ruse that everything in my world was fine. Still, those around me knew nothing of our family's new awful secret.

Joe and Sarah, on the other hand, seemed more comfortable with each passing day. Joe seemed pleased. In his mind, he could have his cake and eat it too. Now in addition to a wife and children, he had a mistress in his home. At night, he would linger on the couch with Sarah. He wouldn't come to bed until long after they had spent time together.

Night after night, the same scene played out. In the middle of the night, Joe slithered into bed next to me. As he pulled me close, he whispered affections. Completely disgusted, I responded with rejection.

Joe fumed, "This is why I'm with her. She would never deny me." Joe's sense of entitlement was deplorable. He honestly couldn't fathom why I, his wife, wouldn't reciprocate physical affections when he crawled into bed after being with his lover. I'm not even sure that to this day he realizes how outlandish his behavior had become.

Sarah's visit with us couldn't end soon enough. It wasn't just the awkwardness of hosting her in our home but the fact that during her stay, Joe monitored my every move with a new vigor. He harshly criticized me, saying I wasn't hospitable enough to Sarah. One afternoon Joe cornered me with his criticism.

"You are ruining her visit with your attitude, Susan," Joe accused.

"What are you talking about? I have been beyond reasonable. And, she's not even my guest. She's yours!" I argued.

"You haven't been kind, and you certainly haven't been hospitable. She doesn't feel welcome here anymore."

"Joe, if she doesn't feel welcome here, maybe it's her own guilt tormenting her," I shot back, unsure how she or Joe could possibly expect any more from me.

"You owe her an apology for ruining her trip. She paid to come visit us and you've made her feel awful."

"Joe, *she* is not the one owed an apology!"

"Well, she and I had a long talk about all of this earlier today. With her trip ending soon, we've decided that she's going to come back during the summer. This trip didn't turn out the way she had hoped," Joe said firmly.

"Joe, she's not coming back this summer!"

"Yes, she is. And because you've ruined this trip, the time she took as vacation, when she comes back, I want to take her away for a few days to make it up to her."

I heard the words that Joe spoke, but I couldn't comprehend what he was saying. His audacity was beyond remarkable. And just when I thought I had found the limits of his crazy thoughts, he found a way to go above and beyond any previous limit.

"I'm going to need your help figuring out where I should take her and help me plan a long weekend away."

I didn't respond to Joe's outlandish request. Instead, in the silence of my reply, he reached for a beer and a cigarette and retreated to our front porch.

I remained alone in the silence for a few minutes, wondering if he was methodically trying to break me down even further than he already had.

HOPE IN THE STORM

B roken and shaken to my core, I had no idea how I could possibly pull myself together to face each day. At home I often tried to hide myself in my favorite role, as mother to Jennifer and Ryan. They always brought a smile to both my face and my heart. They made my life worth living. While spending time with them made me genuinely happy, I knew I couldn't rely on them as my daily source of joy. Heading home after a day at work would bring such mixed emotions—excitement to see my children yet anxiety over what might be waiting for me at home. I often whispered desperate prayers during my commute: *God, please give me the strength to get through today.* Or *Lord, please bless me with Your peace.* I was amazed that prayers so simple could deliver such remarkable strength or result in such unexplainable peace. Some evenings, peace completely washed over my anxious soul, leaving me stress-free.

It didn't make sense to me, given the current turmoil of my marriage, but pondering the immense transformation that often followed my prayers, I was reminded of the closing prayer our pastor had ended

Sunday services with when I was a child. His words, adapted from Philippians 4:7 in the King James Bible: "May the *peace* of God, which *passes all understanding*, go with you." It was a phrase I'd heard week after week, yet until now, the true meaning had escaped me. But as my prayers were answered time and time again, I began to truly find peace.

In addition to my prayers, I continued to listen to the Christian radio station that I had found a few years earlier. My commute became a safe place, free from life's distractions, to learn more about God. Along with my prayers, the programs I listened to provided hope. Between the combination of talk and music programs, I found myself listening out of curiosity, hungry for more of what God had to say.

One program that I began listening to regularly was *In Touch with Dr. Charles Stanley*. Somehow his seemingly effortless sermons brought the Bible to life in a way I had never heard before. His approach was very different from the pastors I had heard growing up. His compelling words drew me into the Bible, leaving me eager to learn more. Not long after I began listening to his programs, I was thrilled to learn Dr. Stanley planned a visit to a venue in my area. My friend Cherie and I attended with great anticipation. Joe said he didn't mind that I went, but did ask our au pair to watch our children. Cherie and I were excited for the opportunity to hear the Bible come to life through Dr. Stanley's words in person.

He didn't disappoint as he told a captivating story from early in his career. He explained that an elderly woman in his church had persistently invited him to visit her home. As a young pastor, he was reluctant, finding himself too busy. She, however, was insistent, so he eventually took the time to visit her. She showed him a large painting of Daniel in the lions' den. Quizzing the young pastor, the woman pressed him for what he saw. Each answer appearing not to be the answer she wanted, she continued to repeat her question. After recanting the many facts and theological views on the story, which illustrated his significant knowledge about Daniel, he still had not mentioned what she saw as the most important aspect of the painting: In the picture, while in the midst of the lions' den, a situation that could have easily caused Daniel his life, Daniel did not focus on the lions. His focus remained instead upon God. Dr. Stanley's illustration left a powerful image in my mind. I couldn't imagine the faith Daniel must have had to stand just steps away from hungry lions yet to focus on God rather than lions.

With all the inspiration I had found, it became natural to read my Bible, something that hadn't been a regular part of my life before. As I did, I was amazed how the words leapt off of the pages, speaking to my current struggles. Prayers for peace to cope were answered with Romans 15:13: "May the God of hope fill you with all joy and peace as you trust in him, so that you may overflow with hope by the power of the Holy Spirit." I couldn't believe how the words soothed my soul and gave me hope in the midst of a situation that seemed so hopeless. What amazed me more than the words of this Bible passage is that I found so many passages that poured strength into my weak and weary soul. The pages of the Bible became a beacon, shining light into my darkness. When I stumbled upon amazing passages that reached out to me, the timing was always impeccable.

Without knowledge of the Bible, outside of God's intervention, I would have had no way of finding such words to speak to my soul when I needed them most. I read, "We will stand in your presence before this temple that bears your Name and will cry out to you in our distress, and you will hear us and save us" (2 Chronicles 20:9). While my spirit continued to be fed by Scriptures that amazed me with their poignant ability to reach me exactly where I was, I also found my network of friends at work slowly growing. In my office, a small group began periodically meeting at lunch to pray or study the Bible. And beyond my coworkers in my building, I began establishing a friendship with a new coworker in our Atlanta office, Mary. I met her when my job shifted to a new project based out of her office. She had a similar job to mine and had been collocated with the rest of my team down south. Although we worked in offices in different states, we hit it off right away. While we didn't immediately talk about faith, her compassion and grace was conveyed over the phone and through e-mails. She, like my new lunch group, seemed to embrace life with such a contagiously positive attitude.

My faith-filled coworkers provided me a new source of strength, while I continued to drink in Scripture that completely amazed me. From a small book of the Bible that I had never heard of before, Lamentations, I read, "Because of the Lord's great love we are not consumed, for his compassions never fail. They are new every morning; great is your faithfulness" (Lamentations 3:22–23). I was truly astounded. Never before had I considered the Bible as anything other than a historical account of stories from the past. But with each new passage, the Bible came to life in a truly unexplainable way. The more I leaned on God, the more He provided the strength I needed to get through each day. This new strength also gave me a new sense of courage that would be essential for me to begin facing the realities of what had become a very difficult situation.

A SHATTERED LIFE

I used the courage that I was beginning to develop to continue seeing my counselor, Molly, over the coming weeks and months. It wasn't easy to pull out the painful pieces of my shattered life, but as I was able, it seemed to provide greater internal strength. As I trusted her more, I opened up more, sharing the bizarre details of my life. Still, I couldn't yet begin to open up about the threats to my safety. Immense fear filled me each time I considered sharing my full story.

In our first session, Molly had outlined certain situations where she would need to break confidentiality. I feared sharing the details of my situation might require her to tell authorities. At the same time, I knew that to ensure my safety, my every move needed to be carefully calculated. The risks of making even one false move were simply too great. It wasn't until much later that I clearly understood that as a counselor, she would have only needed to report a situation if my children were in danger or if I had personally made threats. Driven by fear, I didn't ask for clarification until I was ready.

While I still considered what to share, I felt it was safe to share about Joe's drinking. It was becoming impossible to ignore that Joe had become a heavy drinker. He far surpassed being a social drinker; on weekends Joe drank from early in the morning until he collapsed into bed at night. During the week, he opened his first beer as soon as he returned home from work. With alcohol in the equation, it was as though I was married to two different people: nice, generous Joe and angry, paranoid, controlling Joe. I lived my daily life on eggshells, not knowing which Joe I would come home to. Molly was immensely valuable in providing resources to help me on my journey to understanding life with an alcoholic. Without a doubt, Al-Anon—an anonymous support group for friends and families of people with drinking problems—was one of the most beneficial resources she introduced me to.

Longing for hope to deal with any piece of my truly messed-up life, I looked online for an Al-Anon group that could work for me. I was surprised that I didn't have to go far; a group met at lunchtime near my work. *Perfect*, I thought. Joe would be none the wiser. I knew he would be enraged at the thought of my attending a support group like Al-Anon. He had made his thoughts all too clear about keeping family matters private.

When I pulled in to the parking lot, I looked around. *Who attends a group like this? Will they be like me?* I wondered. Never having been exposed to alcoholism when I was growing up, I had absolutely no idea how many others lived in its murky shadows. I would soon learn, behind closed doors, that many others were suffering too.

"Welcome. Is this your first time?" a lady asked, breaking the continuous flow of racing questions in my head. She reached out her hand to shake mine. With her other hand she reached for a packet of information and a small book on the table next to her. She handed both to me, inviting me to find a seat in the large chair circle to her right.

I was nervous. *What will they be like? Will they understand? Will I have to talk?* Questions continued to swirl in my head. The next hour passed quickly. Relieved that I didn't have to share, I was surprised by how much I gained from listening as others shared bits of their stories. More than anything, I was amazed that a group of total strangers could describe daily occurrences in their lives, almost as if they knew my own trials.

Listening to the others share, I realized we had much in common. The strangers around the Al-Anon circle that day described the feeling that they too lived on eggshells not knowing which next move would trigger their loved one into a tirade or an alcoholic binge. Although it was but one aspect of my difficult situation, finding people who understood a portion of it was liberating. Over the coming weeks, I attended several more meetings and even gained the strength to share.

Despite this new strength, I wasn't yet ready to open up, to call what I was dealing with abuse. Although in my mind I knew, I wasn't ready to give it a name. I had no visible scars, only internal pain.

Over weeks of seeing Molly, I realized the sessions were slowly allowing me to understand the puzzle pieces of my life. Before, I had thought I knew what all of the pieces were and I just wanted strength to deal with the mess I was living in. Secretly I had hoped for a quick-fix answer that would make my life better. Surely there must be some way to help Joe stop drinking and end his infidelity while helping him decide to focus on our marriage. While I didn't find a quick fix, counseling helped me begin to deal with the pieces of my life truthfully. Through it, I began to realize the extent to which I relied on denial, sometimes daily, to suppress the pain of living with an alcoholic, angry, unfaithful husband. Denial allowed me to push my pain into dark shadowy corners of my life, a survival technique I subconsciously used for years. I walked on eggshells thinking if I did enough, if I tried harder, if I was a better wife, a better mother, Joe would change. Broken, I had become a shadow of my former self, now lacking even the confidence I had when I had first met Joe. Ironically, it was Joe's words of acclamation that once built me up. Now, just a few years later, it was his words that tore me down. My heart ached. Though I was truly beginning to see my situation as abuse, I still struggled to call it that.

Joe himself bragged that he was the one in his family to have broken the cycle of abuse. Abused by his father, he vowed to never continue the cycle. Convinced he had been successful, he sang his own praises, celebrating that he had never once laid a hand on me—the absence of bruises a victory to Joe. I was tormented by this distinction. How could I be in so much pain? How could this hurt so much and not be considered abuse?

Joe's extreme kindness and generosity always followed the worst of our conflicts. These honeymoon periods that followed each episode could last for months and made it even easier to question my inner pain. How could I quantify something I couldn't see? My thoughts weren't logical, but I found myself thinking that if I had bruises, maybe it would be easier to admit that the line had been crossed. If I could see my pain, would it be harder to ignore? If I could see the damage he caused, somehow it seemed as though it would be easier to admit it to myself. Looking back, I'm reminded of how bad it must have been to think such distorted thoughts. Joe's abuse never escalated to such physical violence, however, and I'm grateful for that.

Even with the extent of the damage already done, I was still willing to work with him to restore our marriage. I revisited the idea of marriage counseling with Joe. I begged him to attend. I hoped counseling could be a mirror, allowing him to see how his choices were destroying us and our family. Joe, however, was abundantly clear; under no circumstances would he be willing to participate in marriage counseling.

"If you were a better wife," Joe offered, "we wouldn't need counseling. In fact, I only drink to escape from you. If you changed, if you were a better wife, I'd quit drinking!"

Joe's ridiculous monologue continued, "Why should I tell a counselor everything I've already told you?" he asked. "You don't change when I tell you how to change, so if you change because a counselor tells you the same thing, I'll resent you."

This same conversation replayed several times over the coming months. At one point, Joe proposed a different ending to our dialog, a suggestion that he thought could strengthen our marriage and help him end his affair. "You should make Sarah your best friend. Figure out what makes her tick. Together, you two are the perfect wife. If you became more like her, I wouldn't need her."

I couldn't believe his audacity. Who suggests such a thing? Part of me wondered what Sarah would think of his suggestion. I'm sure she wouldn't have appreciated his creativity. That was a moot point; I wasn't following through on his suggestion. Even so, while she was thousands of miles away, the topic of Sarah regularly fueled arguments between us. Because of the distance Joe was unable to be physically intimate with her, but it became apparent that his emotional tie to her was deepening. They spent many nights talking, sharing the details of their lives from afar.

As innocent as conversation can be, I could see how it was leading to a very deep level of emotional intimacy between Joe and Sarah. One night after an argument over how much time the two of them spent on the phone together, Joe reached a new low. "I want to have a child with Sarah," he blurted out, his heavy words dropping like a brick on the floor between us.

They were words I did not want to touch, an open invitation to an argument at a whole new level. I chose not to accept the invitation. I was done arguing. But that night Joe seemed determined to pick a fight. My silence seemed to fuel his anger. "You're going to be nice to her when she comes back, right?" he demanded, his tone harsh.

"I'm not going to take care of her, Joe. She's not my guest," I responded, quickly angering him.

He paused, took a deep breath, and launched into a soliloquy. "I have always been here for you. When you took your job, you knew you would have to travel. You've had to travel a lot here or there, and I have always been here for you. Everything you've ever wanted, I've given you. Now I need your support, and you won't give it. You aren't being fair, Susan. I need to have your word that you'll be nice toward her."

Stunned, I drew every ounce of strength I could to respond. "I'm not going to take care of her. She is not my guest."

Joe, visibly angry, gulped a big swig from his beer can and demanded, "You *will* be nice to her when she comes back. Period." Arguments like this were like brushfires. They typically appeared suddenly. Often they burn hard and fast, quickly fizzling. Other times, they rage. Regardless, I felt doomed to continue arguing about her visit until her return.

I vividly remember one night when the evil Joe returned with a vengeance. It seemed like just another night when I had rolled into bed angry and broken. Joe stayed up late that night, listening to music and drinking beer. I woke up when he finally came to bed around midnight, but pretended to be asleep. I'd had enough arguing earlier that day. I was done dealing with him for the night.

Joe, on the other hand, came to bed with entirely different intentions. As he rolled into bed, he slid his arm around me and pulled me close. Eyes still closed, I cringed inside. Still angry from our argument, I felt disgust and betrayal flowing through my veins as Joe inched closer.

"Joe, stop," I said, acknowledging his advances while letting him know I was definitely not interested. "I'm trying to sleep. It's late and I have to work in the morning."

Joe pulled himself closer. "She would never deny me. You know?" he said, his voice stern and forceful. "You're my wife."

I could feel his body pressing against me as he pulled me even closer.

"Joe, stop," I insisted. "I'm not in the mood. I want to sleep." I could not separate myself from the argument of earlier. I knew that Joe's thoughts were consumed by Sarah. He had said so much. Knowing that, no part of me wanted to be intimate with him; the same person who wanted to be physically intimate with me wanted to have a child with his mistress and planned to kill me if I tried to leave. None of this added up to intimacy for me.

Joe ignored my plea, forcing himself on me.

I began to sob loudly. Between my sobs, I begged him to stop. With one final plea, "Please, Joe, stop!" he slapped a pillow over my face and said, "Be quiet."

The entire episode was over in a matter of a few minutes, although it felt like hours. I pressed my face into my pillow, still soaking from the flood of tears. Numb, I curled up, all too happy to fall asleep where I could escape the pain.

GATHERING PROOF

Daydreaming became a wonderful respite, offering a welcomed distraction from my daily life. It was an easy, temporary escape to get lost in thoughts that a new life could really be possible. But looking at my situation, I realized that from the outside, Joe appeared to be the model spouse, father, and member of society. I had absolutely no proof that Joe wasn't the prefect husband everyone thought he was. The neighbors were endeared by his unending generosity. If anyone needed anything, Joe gladly helped. I think he truly would have given the shirt off his own back if anyone had asked.

The disconnect between appearance and reality troubled me. *God, if I have no proof*, I prayed, *how am I ever going to break free from this life? Please help me find the proof I need.* I had no idea what I expected for an answer. I'm not even sure I really knew what I was asking. I just knew I needed God's help.

Following my plea, life continued. A few days went by, and as on so many other occasions, I began unloading industrial-sized groceries from a warehouse store. Almost as soon as I had begun, I was interrupted by Joe. He rushed out of the house, yelling, meeting me at the back of my van. Sputtering, he began to verbally unload on me. While I had been was gone, he'd looked into one of his credit card accounts. Fearing I had paid it late, he was enraged. He assumed I intended to pay the bill late as a personal affront to him, and his anger now focused on me. He slammed his martial-arts-trained fist into the back inside panel of my van just past my head, splitting the hard plastic and cutting his hand. Cursing, he took a step back and kicked the enormous laundry detergent box I had set down on the driveway. He grunted in pain, fuming at me one more time, before disappearing into the house, leaving me in the driveway with our oversized groceries.

An hour later, Joe hobbled into the kitchen. "I think I need to go to the doctor. I think I broke something. Can you call and see if they're still open?"

Looking up in disbelief, I picked up the phone and dialed. Given the limited Saturday hours, we knew it would be a long shot to get an appointment. After only a few rings, one of the nurses answered. "My husband hurt his hand and his foot," I said. "He thinks he may have broken something. Is there someone who can see him?"

There was a brief pause on the other end of the phone. "He injured his hand and his foot?" she questioned.

"Yes," I responded.

She paused again and then spoke. "Are you okay?"

In an instant I realized this could be some subtle proof of Joe's anger. "Yes," I responded.

"Could you be here in a half hour?"

"Yes, that works."

Just a short while later, the doctor attended to Joe's injuries. Reaching for a bandage in the cupboard behind Joe, she made eye contact with me and mouthed, "Are you okay?" Although I responded with a nod, I felt reassured that someone else *knew*.

Despite my nod to the doctor, I still hadn't found the courage to verbally share the extent of my situation with anyone. In time, I continued to share more with Molly, but I still didn't have the courage to tell my family or friends. It was as though I was living in a prison with invisible bars, bars only I could see. I knew God was the only One who knew everything, so I continued to pray on a daily basis for strength, provision, and guidance.

A few weeks after Joe's injury, another Saturday brought an additional answer to prayer. Cherie stopped by for an unplanned visit. It was out of the ordinary for her to do that. Despite having been friends for a few years, we typically visited at work or over lunch. Knowing that Joe could be unpredictable, I rarely invited friends over to the house. On that Saturday, we had barely settled into a conversation on the couch when the phone rang. A man's voice asked to speak with Joe.

"Who is it?" he asked as he reached for the phone.

"I don't know," I said, handing Joe the receiver.

Over the next few minutes, Joe exploded in anger, arguing intensely. Although we could hear only one side of the conversation, it was obviously quite heated. Only after Joe hung up did we learn both sides of the odd conversation.

The man who called had found Joe's name and phone number in his girlfriend's pocket. Convinced she was having an affair with Joe, he had called to confront Joe. Angered by what he said were false accusations, Joe was furious. He said that at first he had struggled to figure out who the man was even talking about. Then, through their conversation, he realized she was a customer-service representative from an airline. On a recent business trip, the airline had lost Joe's luggage. He said he had never even met the woman in question. Her boyfriend, consumed with a jealous rage, found Joe's name and number on a piece of paper she had apparently left in her pocket when she left work. The man's rage was met with anger equal to his own.

Joe hung up the phone and responded in a way only I had witnessed before. With Cherie sitting next to me within earshot of Joe, we heard his angry, loud conversation as he called his "contact" from years ago. Furious that anyone would call our home and talk to him like that, Joe was determined to teach the man a lesson. This was a side of Joe no one else whom I trusted had ever seen before, but now—sitting on the couch in my home—Cherie couldn't avoid witnessing all. We sank into the couch, shocked, as we overheard Joe's disturbing discussion.

I excused myself from my conversation to join Joe in the kitchen. "It was an honest mistake," I pleaded. "Joe, please let it go."

"He needs to pay, Susan. No one talks to me like that," Joe snarled.

"Please, Joe."

"Do you know who I am? He needs to know who he's dealing with. No one calls my home and speaks to me like that," Joe continued.

"Please don't do anything, Joe. Please!" I begged.

"I'll think about it. But I won't promise you anything," Joe said.

Cherie left not long after Joe got off the phone. Neither one of us was sure of what to make of the situation.

It was only after relentless begging later that night that Joe finally called off his plans. How could a simple case of lost luggage turn into such a potentially dangerous situation? I felt sick to my stomach. With my stomach still churning, I was reminded of my prayer. *God, if I have no proof, how am I ever going to break free from this life? Please help me have proof.*

In a whisper to my soul, God said, *I am giving you proof. I will be faithful to provide all that you need.*

SHARING THE BURDEN

A few months into my weekly meetings with Molly, I finally decided I could trust her with my entire story. My lunch-hour appointments had become a respite from the chaos of my life. Leaving her office that day, after telling her everything, I felt a thousand pounds lighter. My situation had not changed in that hour, but I truly felt as though I no longer needed to carry the burden of my truth alone. It was powerfully liberating. Through our conversation, I decided that it was time to talk to an attorney. While I desperately fought the idea of divorce, I knew I needed to know my options. After much consideration, I carefully chose a Christian attorney, one I thought shared my values. I hoped for answers, for support, and, most of all, for options for my future.

I was filled with anxiety and cautious optimism heading into my first meeting. When I arrived, I was ushered into a large conference room with an oblong wooden table facing a floor-to-ceiling bookcase filled with law books. A few minutes later, a tall, distinguished gentleman with salt–and-pepper hair, wearing a dark suit joined me at the table, taking a seat across from me. He introduced himself as an attorney at the firm. As I began sharing the details of my situation, he filled the large yellow legal pad in front of him with notes. Occasionally he looked up and asked a question about something I had shared. I responded and continued. Before I finished, I explained that I was paralyzed with fear because of the plans already outlined by Joe to ensure I would never get away from him alive. Compassion washed over his face, letting me know he realized the severity of my situation. Shortly after, I finished recounting the sordid details. I hoped to hear the simple phrase, "I can help you."

Instead, he looked down at his notepad, paused before breaking the silence, and said, "After hearing your situation, I am not the right attorney for you. Your case is not the type of case I am equipped to handle."

I was stunned. Any hope I had pulled together to form the ounce of optimism I had previously clung to burst into a million pieces in that instant. As though he knew I needed a moment to recover from my shock, he paused before recommending I seek out the services of an attorney who specifically had experience with domestic-violence situations. Tearing off a corner of a piece of his paper, he scrawled the name of another law firm on it. Then he pushed the scrap of paper across the table toward me. Extending his hand to shake mine, he said, "Good luck. I hope they are able to help you."

I curled the paper up in my hand. Picking up my keys and purse, I thanked him for his time before heading to my car, dejected. The number stayed in my hand, even as I drove. I couldn't risk putting the paper into my pocket or my purse. I knew it could not accidentally find its way home. I returned to work and tucked the piece of paper in a drawer, unsure if anyone would ever really be able to help me.

In the days to come, I drifted between hoping things would change, wanting to pretend life could be okay, and wanting to be free to live a "normal" life. I knew pursuing change would be a marathon. There wasn't a quick fix. Having combed through Web sites, I was disheartened by the startling statistics. One statistic in particular haunted me: 75 percent of all deaths attributed to domestic violence occur after the victim leaves the relationship. The journey would require endurance, perseverance, and a tremendous amount of trust in God.

At two o'clock on a Saturday morning, my conviction to pursue a new life solidified. Startled out of a deep sleep, I awoke to Jennifer's bloodcurdling screams. I quickly rushed to her to see what was wrong.

Sobbing hysterically, she was sitting with her knees curled up, hugging them. "Mommy!" she exclaimed as I entered her room. She threw her arms around me, clenching tightly as I sat down on the side of her bed. "I dreamt that Daddy made you go to heaven." Tears welled in her eyes as she looked up to meet my gaze. The hope I'd had that my children were oblivious to our struggles or the danger I found myself in was shattered. Deep down, my sweet little six-year-old girl knew.

Now that I knew she knew, I could no longer pretend otherwise. Sitting there, hugging Jennifer, I couldn't say, "It's okay, Daddy would never do that." Internally, I shared the same fear. Instead, I hugged her back and said, "Mommy's right here, and I love you very much."

Over the next week, Jennifer had the same nightmare two additional times. My resolve solidified each time. I needed to put change into effect. Fast.

The following Monday, I found the courage to call the second attorney from my office. His office wasn't too far from work, which made a lunch appointment possible. I pulled into the parking garage, scanning my rearview mirror. I continued cautiously, looking around for any movement or suspicious people or cars. Not convinced Joe wouldn't be watching me at lunch, I knew the inherent risk of pulling into a large legal building's parking garage. I hurried into the building, quickly ducking into the elevator.

With a swift movement, the door chimed, opening on the sixth floor to an impressive-looking law firm. "May I help you?" the receptionist asked before my eyes finished scanning the lobby.

"Hello, I'm Susan. I have an appointment today," I said.

"Oh yes, I see you're meeting with Mr. Smith. Please have a seat and I'll let him know you're here," she said motioning to the waiting area. "Can I get you a coffee or water?"

"No, thank you," I said, taking a seat next to the coffee table covered with magazines and newspapers. I glanced over the headlines of the *Washington Post* and the *New York Times*. But my nerves were too on edge to focus on anything. *Dear God, please let Mr. Smith help me,* I prayed, seeking to calm my racing thoughts. *And please protect me.* But before I could finish my prayer or collect my thoughts, the receptionist's voice broke my train of thought. "Your appointment is here," she said into the phone, informing Mr. Smith of my arrival before returning to the work on her desk.

A few minutes later, Mr. Smith walked up to me. "Welcome," he said, shaking my hand. He ushered me down the hall into a room with law books filling shelves from floor to ceiling. We sat down at the large conference table much like I had done at the other law office. He pulled out a yellow legal pad, jotting details as I recounted my situation. Asking only a few questions, he let me do much of the speaking at this initial meeting. When I finished, I waited for his reaction.

He looked down over the notes scrawled on his pad and then looked up. "I'd be happy to work with you," he told me.

A sense of relief washed over me. I didn't have to face this alone.

I met with Mr. Smith several times over the coming weeks, each time focusing on different details of my situation. It quickly became apparent that he had worked with cases similar to mine in the past because he thought of many things I had not even considered. At one of our initial meetings, he suggested I try to find a way to document the excessive amounts of alcohol Joe consumed. He cautioned me to be very careful, knowing the potential danger if Joe found out.

In the beginning, I tried separating Joe's beer cans from other trash. For a week at a time, I put the cans in a separate bag hidden in our garage. At the end of the week, I unloaded the bag, took a picture to document the totals before taking them to the end of the driveway, and tucked them in with our other trash. It didn't take long to establish a careful routine that seemed to be working well.

At the end of the third week, the beer can bag was bursting in the garage, waiting for the next day's trash collection. When I got home from work that day, I followed my typical routine and began preparing dinner for our family. As my preparations began, within my thoughts a voice whispered, *Move the bag.*

Caught off guard, I paused, looking around, confused. Unable to make sense of what I thought I'd heard, I continued working on dinner. I no sooner began cooking when the voice inside me spoke again, *Move the bag! Now!*

This time there was a clear sense of urgency. Since I was alone in the kitchen, the source of the voice made no sense. I rationalized that the bag was stored in a part of the garage that Joe didn't typically disturb, plus he wasn't even home from work yet. Still, feeling an overwhelming sense of urgency, I immediately went to the garage and moved the bag to a different spot, tucked away next to some random items stored in bins.

I turned to head back into the kitchen when I heard Joe's voice outside. He was talking to one of our neighbors, and they were quickly approaching the house. As soon as I returned to my dinner preparations, Joe and our neighbor appeared in the kitchen.

"I'll be right back," Joe said to our neighbor. He passed through the kitchen to the garage. Returning moments later, Joe was holding hedge trimmers that we rarely used. They had been hanging on the wall directly above where the beer can bag had been only moments earlier.

I exhaled a long, slow breath, amazed at how narrowly I had averted danger. There could have been no logical explanation that I could have crafted that would have satisfied Joe that day had I not moved the bag. I shook my head in amazement. Clearly, God was looking out for me. Over the coming weeks, I continued to document Joe's alcohol consumption at the recommendation of my attorney. God was faithful to protect my efforts.

As an additional step in documenting my situation, my attorney also recommended I hire a private investigator. "A lot of people say they want to kill someone. Most often, they don't really mean it," he shared. "We need to know which situation you're dealing with." A private investigator could provide insight into the risks and dangers should I attempt to leave Joe. The lawyer recommended a local company used by some of his other clients. Unsure how I could afford the investigator, or how I could set aside that amount of money without Joe's noticing, I confided in trusted family members. "I promise, one day I'll pay you back," I vowed. Understanding the severity of my situation, I don't think their first concern was my ability to eventually pay them back. With the money in hand, the wheels were in motion.

A few days later, lunchtime again found me slipping out of work to attend a meeting, this time with a private investigator. I turned into the mostly residential neighborhood before pulling in to the narrow driveway, which led to a parking lot behind an unassuming little house. It really didn't look like much from the outside, but I'm sure that was their intent. The parking lot, neatly tucked around the back of the building, wasn't visible from the road in front.

On the inside, I was transported into a scene from a movie. Several small offices connected to the main corridor. Each office looked exactly like what my mind would conjure if I recalled a private investigator's office from the big screen. The receptionist greeted me and then introduced me to one of the PIs. He ushered me into his small office and then sat down behind an oversized wooden desk, which housed a large desktop computer and an in-box bursting with files and papers. I slipped into the wooden chair facing him. The bright midday sun made the window shade behind his desk glow warmly. The pulled shade appeared to cover a large window directly behind his chair. I wondered if he pulled it because of the glare it might have caused on his computer or to protect the anonymity of clients like me.

Over the next half hour, I recounted many of the details of my life. With each additional detail, my life sounded more like a suspenseful and dramatic movie than the life of a middle-class, sub-urban mom. I described Joe's chilling plans, including who he would employ as well as his alibi, detailing how he would get away with it all. As I spoke, the man scribbled notes on a small spiral tablet. Occasionally, he looked up and asked a clarifying question before his focus returned to the pad in front of him. Oddly, I found the visit re-assuring. No, my situation hadn't changed, but I realized I was most definitely no longer alone. Now several others knew my details. At a minimum, I knew if anything did happen to me, justice would have a greater chance.

Several weeks passed before I returned to that small house. In the time since my first visit, the investigator had researched Joe's plan through his own resources, with the intent to uncover as much as pos-sible about Joe's background and who his connections really were. Un-sure of what to expect, I was filled with a variety of emotions, hope and fear the most prevalent.

I entered the house and was once again guided into the same small office. The private investigator who had so feverishly taken notes joined me. As he settled into the chair opposite me, he set down a large manila folder on the desk between us. The folder was plump—a large stack of papers bursting out of it.

He cleared his throat and began. "In my line of work, people often say phrases such as, 'I'm going to kill you.' We find, typically, in more than 90 percent of the cases, it's just hot air." He paused. "In about 10 percent of the cases, we say the threat needs to be taken very seriously." He paused again, glanced down at the folder, and then looked back up and made eye contact with me before continuing. "I am so sorry; you are in the 10 percent."

I sank in my chair. Deep down, I had already known my fear was founded. I hoped, however, that maybe there could be a chance I was wrong. I desperately wanted to be wrong. The investigator opened the bursting folder and began flipping through the pages before him. In Joe's eagerness to keep me imprisoned by fear, he had provided generous details of his meticulously thought-out plan, including who he would employ. Since our first meeting, the investigator had completed a background check on both Joe and his associates. For the most part, they had been the mysterious voices on the other end of the phone in the past. On a few rare occasions his associates came to our house. Joe told me many times that he tried to keep "business" away from our family. Now, the history of a checkered past spilled out of the plump folder onto the table before me. The pages detailed a history that removed all doubt; I had reason to fear Joe and his associates. *You are in the 10 percent,* echoed in my mind. There would be no quick fix for my situation. Instead, a careful plan needed to evolve. Every step of my journey became more serious, more focused, and absolutely necessary. My life depended on it.

That night, I walked through our home with a different set of eyes. I looked at everything—absolutely everything—we had collected over the years: furniture, photos, toys, TVs, the dining room set that I had always wanted to hold the crystal that I had purchased as an exchange student all those years ago. Years of saving and buying on credit had filled my house with products of a marriage seeking to build a home—a home with my husband. Looking at some of the furniture and items, I could tap into the distant emotions that I had felt when we brought home the very pieces I revisited that night. What of it really mattered? Would I really miss it? Funny how such a full home could feel so empty. My heart physically ached. We had worked so hard to make this house a home. Now it was breaking apart in front of me. Any denial of my reality was shattered first with the vivid nightmares of my daughter followed by the investigator's thorough report. Emotionally, our home already destroyed, I knew it wasn't long before our physical home would follow. It was time for a change. My planning began in earnest.

That night, my life's perspective changed from building the home that I had always wanted, to knowing I would let go of everything I had. My previous focus on maintaining the American Dream became a thing of the past. Empowered by my faith and growing support network, my focus shifted to trusting God and finding a way out. Outside of safety for my children and me, some comforts for my children, and a few family sentimental items, none of it really mattered. On the surface, our house looked like a home. The family room now looked so welcoming—with the once rust-colored shag carpet now blue plush carpet, the kitchen painted, the dining room fully furnished to serve friends and family at holidays and birthday parties. Absolutely every project, every update, had been made with love. Now, none of that mattered. With great conviction, my children and my safety became all that I wanted, all that I really needed.

WEAVING THE NET

O ver the coming weeks, I set the wheels in motion. My thoughts often drifted to planning my escape. One day at lunchtime, I gathered up enough courage to search for online domestic violence resources. Nervously I typed "domestic violence help" in my Internet search box and clicked search quickly, almost as if I was afraid I'd lose the courage if I waited. I knew I needed help, but I had no idea where this path might lead. When a list of sites popped up, I thought, *What will it say? Can they really help?* Before I clicked on the first link, before my thoughts could race any further, the site came up on my screen. Boldly displayed at the top of the page was a toll-free hotline number. My eyes fixed on the number. *I need to memorize this number, just in case,* I thought. Then my eyes nervously scanned the page. "Is it abuse?" the first link asked. Although I knew the answer, knew Joe wasn't anywhere around, I still glanced over my shoulder, my heart racing, before looking back and clicking on the link.

The site returned a list of traits of abusive relationships. With each line I read, my heart sank a bit deeper. Although my doubt and denial had become impossible to hold on to after recent developments, the list still captivated me. It was hauntingly familiar, almost as if whoever wrote it knew me, knew Joe, and knew the hell I had been living through. After saying yes to the first several traits on the list, I clicked on the header Get Help as I looked over my shoulder again, feeling not just anxious but somewhat guilty too.

The site outlined how to create a safety plan to leave an abusive relationship. As I read the site, I began taking careful notes, wanting to be sure I did everything I needed to do. Too much depended upon it. Over the coming days, I continued to use lunchtime and other breaks to explore valuable online resources that provided information for victims of domestic violence, which helped me to carefully consider important details while ensuring I didn't forget any vital steps in the process. I was careful to never access any sites from home, only at work. I didn't want to chance any trails being left in my online history. One of my first steps was to identify the critical documents I would need and to be sure not to leave anything behind, such as birth certificates, passports, and tax returns. I was surprised that many of the Web sites I found listed key documents for this very purpose. I don't know if I would have ever thought of documents such as tax returns without the site's valuable help. Even after my initial research, I knew my actions would require organization. I kept a folder at work with a list and my notes so I wouldn't forget anything critical. I drew a purple ribbon on the upper right corner of the folder so that it wouldn't get confused with any of my work files. Visiting the online sites, I had learned that the purple ribbon was the color for domestic violence awareness. Somehow I knew that for me the color purple would never be the same. It now meant hope for me because I knew that I wasn't the first one who needed to take these scary steps. And, out there, beyond my own little world, there were entire organizations available to help me.

At home, I began pulling the documents into a central location in our filing cabinet. Document by document, I organized each piece on the list. In addition, I took great care to pay all of our bills and set aside cash that I knew I would later need. I was careful to set aside a small amount with each paycheck over several weeks so that it didn't visibly impact our household finances.

A key part of my plan was to identify a target date. Through discussions with my attorney and the private investigator, we identified a goal date to leave with the children. With summer approaching and Sarah scheduled to return, we knew Joe's focus would shift to her. He still believed I was paralyzed by fear, too weak to consider running, a perception I could use in my favor. Joe and Sarah's plans to go on vacation had been hijacked by a conference at Joe's job. He decided that instead of the two of them going on vacation, they could travel to his conference in Texas together. The trip would give them the time alone they sought. The trip would also give me the perfect opportunity to leave.

The date was picked. I would leave while they were far away in Texas. I realized, however, while I had picked a "move" date, there would be no guarantees I would be able to wait until that day. Sarah's approaching visit stirred Joe's emotions. His unstable emotions coupled with bursts of intense anger caused me to create a plan B. I read on several domestic violence Web sites that a secondary plan is advised, in the event that my situation should become too dangerous to stay in. It wasn't something I really wanted to consider; after all, it was hard enough thinking about leaving at all. Still, no one was the wiser.

I cleared out most of the items in the credenza in the corner of my office at work, making space for one lone duffle bag. Tucked in the bag was one change of clothes for my children and me, toothbrushes, a couple of small toys, cash, and a few essentials. In time I added our critical documents to the bag. We were ready to run with only the essentials if we absolutely needed to.

As my plans developed, it became essential to confide in a few trusted friends. I prayed for wisdom to know whom I could trust. I knew my life depended upon my developing plan. Without a doubt, I could not afford to tell the wrong person. After careful consideration, I decided to tell two trusted friends, Cherie and Mary. Cherie had seen Joe's wrath. I knew she would quickly understand the true danger I faced. Her love for my children as well as me proved to be a valuable source of strength. Words cannot describe how much it meant to me to have someone who—in the depths of my valley—prayed with me, encouraged me, and was just there to support me.

The second person I told was Mary. Through work, I had gained a tremendous amount of respect for her. Although she lived over a thousand miles away, her incredible faith, compassion, and strong ethics were visible daily through her work. I felt it important to let her know about my struggles as well as my plans for escape. Never could I have fathomed her response. Knowing the dangers of my situation, Mary offered her home as a refuge without hesitation. No words will ever be able to adequately express my gratitude to her for providing us a home when we desperately needed a safe place to reside. Now we had a goal date to leave, and we had someplace to go. My plans were taking shape.

Despite my focus on these imminent plans, my daily charade with Joe continued. He was keenly aware that I really didn't want to entertain Sarah for yet another visit, yet the two of them solidified the plans for her lengthy stay. Initially they hoped she could spend a few weeks with us, with some of the time devoted to their vacation together. As much as I did not want to host Sarah, I knew her arrival and presence would provide sufficient distraction for Joe, allowing the final preparations and implementation of my plans to unfold.

While I had opened up to two close friends and a few others, I still had not shared my drama with other friends or family. Sarah's return gave me an opportunity to slip away with Jennifer and Ryan to visit my parents in Pennsylvania. Leaving Joe and Sarah for the weekend at our home might have seemed an odd choice, but it was strategic. Joe assumed my trip was planned to wish my mother well as she prepared for major surgery. While that was no doubt part of my agenda, I had an even bigger agenda. In addition to the opportunity to share my plans with my family, the trip would also provide my private investigator the opportunity to document Joe and Sarah's affair. With the two of them staying at our home, there would likely be some displays of affection that could later prove Joe's infidelity. I knew proof of that would help me when I filed for divorce.

The several-hour drive to my parents' house that June morning seemed to my children like any of the countless past trips we'd taken to their grandparents. It was uneventful in their innocent eyes. To my parents, awaiting our arrival, nothing was out of the ordinary. "Let us know when you're on your way," my mom would typically request. This trip was no different. To me, however, this trip was anything but ordinary. Not knowing our future, not knowing the turns it might take,

I ventured homeward with a single intent. I wanted desperately to hug each of them one more time and tell them how much I loved them. This trip was to say good-bye.

We arrived to the warm, welcoming hugs of my parents. Within moments, my children slipped into the next room. I heard the familiar *clink* of a glass lid, and knew they had found their nana's candy jars once again. No doubt they were filled and right where she always left them, placed at just the perfect height for grandchildren. It made me smile, warmly remembering all the times my grandmother did the same for me at her house. A twinge of sadness came over me. This was one of the sweet, warm family traditions we'd be leaving behind.

I soaked in everything that day, as though writing every possible detail to memory with permanent ink. I didn't want to forget a single sight, sound, or moment. It was such a wonderful day—filled with all the typical things we loved to do together. One of our favorite stops was the local candy store because no trip to visit my parents was ever complete without the absolute best chocolate-covered pretzels.

Back at my parents' house, my dad gave Jennifer and Ryan rides on his big, red, old Farmall tractor. It was something he did often, sharing part of his own past. And no trip to my parents would ever be complete without my mother's fussing over us at dinner. Every part of that June day, every ordinary, common element, those moments typically taken for granted, was a treasured gift.

At night, after my children were tucked in bed, I slipped back downstairs. There, my parents were enjoying their nightly routine of watching a news program, my mom sipping hot tea on the sofa, my dad tucked in his recliner, struggling to stay awake.

"Do you have a minute?" I asked. I sat down next to my mom. Both my words and tone grabbed their attention. "Of course," Mom said as Dad turned off the TV. They could tell I was about to share something serious. How serious, I'm sure, was nothing they could have predicted.

Over the next several hours, I walked them through the months leading up to that moment. I shared my plans to flee and the very real threats against us. My heart broke as I let them know Joe's additional threats against their safety. Together, we cried. Wishing it were just a Monday night movie that we could simply turn off, we were left with only the option to deal with the challenges that lay ahead. Together we discussed the painful truth, that if anything should happen to them, I could not return; it would be too dangerous. We consoled each other with the depth of emotions that welled up before us.

"When will we see you again?" my mother asked.

"I don't know," I choked out, not knowing if there would be a next time.

The next morning, with my exit plans solidified and just days away, my focus shifted to helping my parents develop a plan to keep them safe. We phoned their local sheriff to discuss the threats to their safety. I knew that leaving Joe put them directly in harm's way, making me determined to do whatever I could to help ensure their safety. Early in the day I facilitated a conversation between the sheriff and my private investigator's office. The background file of information his office held proved to be valuable, helping the local authorities develop their plan. Working together, they quickly solidified a strategy to protect my parents. The police agreed to set up additional patrols over the coming weeks in my parents' neighborhood. With my departure date overlapping my mother's hospital stay, we extended their plan to cover her stay there and included keeping her hospital stay private. Additionally, my father made arrangements to stay away from home while my mother was hospitalized. Then, with the assistance of trusted friends, my parents also decided to stay away from home for the weeks immediately following her release.

After talking through the entire plan, my parents put in place one last precaution. Joe knew how much our family treasured my father's childhood home, where they now lived. It was not outside of Joe's wrath to destroy what I—what we—valued. Knowing their home could also be in danger, my parents carefully selected valued family antiques and moved them to storage until they could be certain the danger had passed. The final step necessary before we returned home was to let my sisters know about my situation. With the love and support of my family, I said good-bye, not knowing if or when I would ever see them again.

LEAP OF FAITH

Our trip back to Maryland was uneventful. Thoughts of my plans consumed my mind so much that I was afraid I might talk in my sleep. Sarah and Joe, who were preparing for their trip to Texas, seemed tense when we returned, as though their time alone hadn't been the wonderful respite they had hoped it would be. Still, a few days later, with roller bags in tow, they said good-bye and headed to the airport. I knew as they left that they had no idea I was about to take control of the messy situation life had become. Just one day later, it was time.

That life-changing June day is but a blur, a necessary step in our journey to a new life. The phone rang early. "What time should we be there? We're ready whenever you are," the voice on the other end said. A few wonderful people in my life became the trusted, faithful few that day. Not everyone with whom I had shared my saga wanted to be part of the solution. I understood that. Knowing Joe's wrath, I knew that anyone who helped me would most definitely be in danger. Certainly I would not wish that on anyone. I wanted no casualties as a result of our exit. In fact, to this day I have never shared with anyone, nor will I, the identity of those who helped me. They know who they are, and I am and will be forever grateful.

"I'm ready," I responded to the voice. It was time.

"Anna," I called to our au pair, "I need to talk to you for a minute." Standing in the foyer of our house, I explained to her much of what led up to this pivotal moment in life. Anna had joined our family the previous summer. She had lived with us six months when Joe confessed his affair. While I don't think she knew all the details of our challenges, I'm certain she picked up on the tension in our home. Anna hung on each word as I shared with her. Today, a new chapter was about to begin. Tears welled in our eyes while Jennifer and Ryan continued to eat their breakfast at the table nearby. Anna and I had the benefit of being able to talk in Swedish because of the time I had spent studying in Sweden. I wanted to make sure my children's young ears did not overhear anything they shouldn't. I wanted to protect them from the disruption of the move. I asked Anna to take them to the park at the end of our street. I also did not want them to know who helped us move. It was simply better if they didn't know.

Anna, Jennifer, and Ryan left minutes later. They spent innocent time together, laughing and playing, before our paths would part. It was an awful way to end Anna's year stay with us. Just weeks away from the official end to her time, I saw no other alternative. She could not come with us. Instead, I made arrangements for her to stay with a friend when we left. I knew the agency that had placed her with us would take care of her from there. I needed to focus solely on the three of us.

Moments after Anna, Jennifer, and Ryan left for the park, my stealthy, faithful movers arrived. They descended on our house like a SWAT team. Not large in number, they were focused on their mission, quickly identifying and loading the things we would take. My plan was not to move the contents of our home but simply to take those items I thought mattered most to me and my children. The next hour was controlled chaos. Jennifer and Ryan's room was dismantled and loaded on to the small U-Haul truck.

Beyond that, the focus remained on sentimental items. We packed up my Swedish crystal from our china cabinet in the dining room, treasures from my year in Stockholm. The beautiful cherry china hutch that I had so valued was left half empty, the hutch and its contents to be left behind.

I turned back to look into the dining room as I grabbed the box I had just packed. It was one of the rooms of our house that had much sentimental value for me. From the time we first bought our townhouse and then this, our single-family home, I had always wanted a dining room. Growing up in a family rich with traditions, the dining room was a gathering place, a family place. Even though our family was breaking apart, it was a room that held fond memories. Now, although it was one of my favorite rooms, I turned away to leave it all behind.

Carefully I worked through each room of the house, taking what I thought were some of the most necessary, yet at the same time some of the saddest, items from our house: every picture of Jennifer, Ryan, and me. I packed our many family photo albums, the boxes of photo negatives, the envelopes of extra prints from all the two-for-one specials, and every last picture and framed photo. I realized the wrenching pain this must have caused Joe, but it was necessary; our safety came before consideration for Joe's sentimental needs. At the direction of my private investigator, we needed to reduce the chances that we could be found. If Joe didn't have pictures of what we looked like, we would increase our chances of successfully getting away. I realize how hard this would be for Joe, but on that day, survival was the sole focus, not compassion.

Not long after we began, the small U-Haul pulled away, taking my stealth team with it. I was left standing in the foyer, heart racing yet fully numb. The packing had been executed with careful precision, exactly to plan. I didn't want anyone to know who helped me because I knew it would be a detail Joe would demand to know. If no one else knew, no one would accidentally slip. I hadn't even considered that someone else, such as a neighbor, might see us.

My team arrived after my children left, and they were gone before the kids returned. In a matter of minutes, Jennifer and Ryan bounced in from the park. My heart truly broke with this, the hardest step of our journey—telling my children that we were leaving, their rooms already packed. I will forever be sorry that I ever needed to so abruptly uproot them. Although I know it was necessary to provide them a better, safer life, it is a burden I will carry for the rest of my life.

My van loaded, it was almost time for us to leave. I walked into the kitchen one last time. Looking around as though taking one last snapshot in my mind, I paused next to the table. I pulled out the stapled set of papers that had been tucked into my purse—my legal request for a divorce—and placed them in the center of the table.

Now there was one final step. Our beloved golden retriever, Alley, could not come with us. Knowing we were about to embrace an uncertain life on the run, I was unsure that I could provide for her. I knew my focus, my priority, needed to be our safety first. With great sadness, the kids and I hugged her good-bye. We carefully tucked her bowls, food, and toys around the side of our house and put her in our backyard. Her big sad brown eyes looked up knowingly at us as if to say good-bye. I gained comfort knowing she would be there for just a few minutes before her new family would swoop in to pick her up. Although I didn't think Joe would hurt her, he wasn't scheduled to be home for days. In addition, I didn't trust what his mental and emotional state would be when he returned, so while I didn't worry he would harm her, I didn't trust he would fully care for her. I knew her new family would shower her with love. Still, leaving her in the backyard and saying good-bye was overwhelmingly heart wrenching.

After years of pain and months of planning, I was really doing this. We were actually leaving. My entire body trembled. With shaking hands, I double-checked Jennifer and Ryan in their seats to make sure they were secure.

Without hesitation, four-year-old Ryan looked up with his big brown eyes and said, "Mommy, you don't have to cry anymore." His sweet words hugged my anxious spirit, confirmation that I really was doing the right thing. His precious words, much like Jennifer's nightmares, reminded me that although I thought I had hidden the conflict, my pain, and my sadness from both of them, they were all too aware.

Pulling out of the driveway, we began a new chapter of our lives. Life would never be the same. Heading out of town, there was one quick stop we needed to make before hitting the open highway—a detour to the private investigator's office.

Knowing Joe's impending rage, I did not want to leave his loaded gun in the house. Instead, keeping it in its case, I took it to the PI's office to be unloaded and locked. When we arrived at the office, the investigators spoke volumes without saying much at all. Their compassion-filled eyes conveyed their concern as they helped with this one last thing before our journey began. They knew the dangers I faced. They knew it wouldn't be easy. Most of all, however, they understood it was necessary.

"Be safe," the first investigator said, leaning forward to hug me.

"Take care of yourself," the other said, extending his hand to me. Then he knelt down to my children's level. "Have a good trip," he said. With a big smile, his eyes met theirs. "Make sure you look for purple cows. I've never seen one, so if you do, you'll have to tell me."

Jennifer and Ryan's eyes grew big. Perplexed, they looked up at me. With those words, we said good-bye.

It was simply not possible to drive far enough away that first day. With every mile marker we passed on the highway, I felt another link in the chain to my old life being broken. I longed to be really free, far from Joe's reach. If it had been physically possible to drive to the other end of the earth that day, I would have found the strength to do just that. Being gone wasn't enough. I longed to be far, far away, completely out of harm's way.

Our total trip would take more than fourteen hours, requiring a long, two-day drive. If Joe didn't know which direction we were headed, I hoped it might feel like the other side of the world to him, and hoped it was indeed far enough. I set my goal of getting at least halfway to our new home on our first day of travel. But the heavy emotions and physical exhaustion from leaving tired me; I was quick to realize my goal was far too lofty.

Instead, we spent the first night a mere four hours from home. Weariness set in and a motel sign on the dark highway beckoned. I pulled in and parked in the little parking lot. I left the kids in the car and ran in to the office. "Do you have any vacancies?" I asked the man sitting at the front desk. I surveyed the lobby as the man stared intently at his computer screen.

"How many nights?" he said with a gruff voice, breaking the long silence.

"Just one," I said.

Looking up as though he was studying me, he replied, "You're in luck. We have one room left. Name?"

Name? Name? What name should I tell him? My heart raced. I knew I couldn't use my real name. I hadn't thought of this detail. What else had I neglected to consider? "Lisa," I blurted out. *Lisa, Lisa,* I thought, racing to pull out a last name. "Lisa Jones." I exhaled. "And I'd like to pay in cash."

"Your room is around back," he said, pointing to the far left. "You'll want to move your car around back."

"Thank you," I said as I picked up the large plastic key ring with our room key.

The old man settled back in his chair. His focus returned to his computer screen, no doubt aware that my name was not Lisa Jones.

I moved the van to the opposite end of the parking lot of the sad-looking motel that would be our home for one night. I wasn't thrilled to be using the back entrance because my mind raced to assess the motel's safety. *Can he find us here? Are we safe?*

The mental interrogation I had begun abruptly stopped as I swung open the door to our motel room. A large octagonal hot tub prominently consumed the far corner of our room. Much to my surprise, the only room available for us was a significant upgrade from the motel's standard fare.

"Whoa!" the kids exclaimed, dropping their bags and running to the not-so-subtle new addition to this room.

Peering over the side, they pleaded, "Can we get in? Can we go swimming?"

What a wonderful, unexpected blessing. On this, the most stressful night of my entire life, either prior or since, a little unassuming motel on the side of the road just so happened to have only one room available, an upgraded suite with wonderful amenities. It was a much-needed and appreciated distraction. "Yes, you can swim," I responded, smiling.

The calm respite our hotel room offered was shattered with the ring of my cell phone. As I turned it over, my heart sank. It was Joe. I ignored it, letting it ring. Over the next hour, he continued to call every few minutes. After the first few calls, I turned my phone off, choosing not to be subjected to the anxiety that came with each call. I decided not to answer any of his calls, not knowing what our conversation might bring.

I listened to the first voice mail. Joe wasn't calling to say goodnight to Jennifer and Ryan; he already knew we were gone. Just hours after our departure, he phoned, frantically pleading that I return home. Through his many messages, his heartbreak was apparent. Despite the fact that he was on a business trip in Texas, he clearly already knew we had left. In his messages, Joe detailed that one of our neighbors, from behind the pulled-back curtains in her own home, had watched us load the U-Haul. She was appalled that a wife would leave her husband while he was away on a business trip, clearly assuming Joe was the victim. Although it took her several hours to reach him, she was persistent. She desperately wanted to make sure he was aware of what was happening at home. She was just one of our many neighbors loyal to Joe, having been wooed by his generosity and charm. The delay she experienced in reaching Joe that day provided the critical time we needed to get away.

Joe's messages were understandably harsh, his anger apparent. The tone in some of his messages sounded desperate and broken, while others were cold, controlling, and calculating. He didn't mince words, nor did he leave doubt about how he knew we had left. He wanted me to know she had carefully watched us. His messages shared that he had drilled her with questions, while she was glad to help, providing every morsel of information she could recall.

There was one specific detail from the beginning that bothered Joe immensely: Who had helped me move? Because of Joe's twisted sense of loyalty, I knew he would focus on this very piece. The neighbor desperately tried to provide specifics and describe the people she saw loading the truck that day. But she had been unable to describe them with enough clarity for Joe to be certain who had helped me. Furious, he felt betrayed by my anonymous helpers. Today I have no doubt their anonymity saved their lives. All these years later, as I share so much of my story with such transparency, it is still a piece of my story that I choose to omit. I am eternally grateful to the few faithful, loyal people in my life who chose to be there when I needed support the most. My greatest act of gratitude toward them is to forever keep their anonymity.

The second day of our journey began with a small breakfast in the hotel lobby. Not surprisingly I woke from restless sleep with no appetite. However, I knew we needed to eat before a long day of traveling. Filled with nervous energy, I desperately longed to be much farther away. It simply wasn't possible to be far enough fast enough for my comfort level. Knowing Joe already knew we were gone fueled my anxiety. So with our quick breakfast, we began the day's journey.

My cell phone rang throughout the day, reminding me of what we were leaving behind. I chose to ignore Joe's calls, though he left irate voice mail after voice mail. Unlike the previous night, I wanted to leave my phone turned on because I wanted to leave the line of communication open for my attorney, the private investigator, and my parents. Their familiar, supportive voices from home as we traveled provided much-needed comfort. Although they didn't know where we were headed, knowing they were out there, still supporting me—us— helped tremendously. Smart phones didn't exist, nor had GPS become available to the general public. Instead, I relied on maps, road signs, and directions. Technology wasn't at all what it is today, which is both good and bad. It was good because the technology of today would have made it harder to disappear. Amber alerts and state-to-state cooperation make finding people faster and easier than ever before. While in most situations this is a very good and even lifesaving thing, for me it would have been devastating. Additionally, the technology of today enables the pinging of cell phones to find a location. I am thankful, for those reasons, my story was before these advancements.

One of the downsides of my old cell phone was that the battery life wasn't designed to last for long days without the advantage of a wall-based charger. Eight hours into our trip, my battery was nearly exhausted.

"Low battery" blinked continually on the screen. My mind raced. My phone was our connection to the world outside my van. Now headed to a new city, I wanted to have the ability to call for directions if we needed to. And I was unwilling to be fully disconnected from my support back home just yet. With only a traditional wall charger and without the access to a wall socket, we would soon be isolated. Desperately wanting to find a solution, I took a random exit on the highway that looked busy with activity. A few gas stations and fast food restaurants prominently advertised their presence just off the ramp. Still with no plan, I was ready for a break from driving. At the end of the ramp, I noticed a shopping plaza and hoped I would figure something out there. What, I wasn't sure. I said a brief prayer for help as my eyes scanned the row of stores and restaurants in the tiny strip mall before I picked a parking spot. Nestled in the middle of the chain of stores, a bright sign beckoned to me. It simply read Christian Bookstore. I don't know what I expected a bookstore to do for me, but somehow it felt safe. *If anyone here can help me, they can,* I thought.

Once in the store, we walked directly up to the register. The lady, busy completing paperwork, looked up. "Can I help you?" she asked.

I proceeded to quietly explain that we were fleeing a dangerous situation and that my cell phone battery was all but gone. Tears welled in my eyes as I spoke. Realizing my request would be extremely unusual, I asked if there was any way she would allow me to charge my phone in their store. Not knowing what other options I really had, I needed to ask. Still at least four hours away from our destination, I knew I could not afford to let my phone's battery completely run down.

Compassion filled her eyes as she agreed to help. For the next half hour, Jennifer, Ryan, and I looked through the fun little things in the children's section while my phone charged. As a welcomed distraction for my children, I let them each pick out a handful of small trinkets. When we paid for our items, the kind stranger handed my cell phone and charger back to me. Soon we were on our way. Somewhere in the south is a friendly Christian bookstore where God used the cashier as His hands that day. I am thankful for her willingness to help a traveler in need.

Several hours later, we pulled off the highway into a strange new town that would become our new home. Rather than navigating unfamiliar roads, we pulled into a parking lot near the highway. Within a few minutes of arriving, my friend and coworker Mary pulled in, greeting us. She was a welcome, friendly face at the other end of our long and emotional trip. She led us back to her home just a short drive away.

Mary lived in a beautiful home in a newly established neighborhood. She moved two of her daughters into one bedroom in order to make room for the three of us in our own private space. A woman I would describe as a grounded, strong, Christian woman, Mary understood the dangers I faced. Despite knowing the potential and very real danger that Joe could find us in that Atlanta suburb, she helped us. She illustrated Christ's love in our lives in a tangible and very personal way. With incredible grace, as a single parent, she worked, provided for her children, and maintained a beautiful home. Her children, also tremendously gracious and kind, shared and demonstrated her values. It could have been challenging or awkward to adjust to a routine while in someone else's home, but Mary and her children made it easy. Through sharing their home and including us in everyday tasks such as grocery shopping and dinner, we quickly adjusted to our new life. We were truly blessed to have been led to such a compassionate home.

Not long after arriving, a national news headline reminded me of just how lucky we were. Both TV and radio programs were consumed with the tragic story of a beautiful young woman who had been killed by her husband. Newscasters rushed to interview the couple's neighbors to get community reactions to the tragedy. "He was the nicest neighbor," one man commented. "He'd do anything for anybody. I never saw anything like this coming," a female neighbor continued, saying she too was shocked. "He's such a nice man," she told the reporter.

Listening to the comments was surreal. I thought about my own situation. Any one of my neighbors back home would have provided the exact same comments. "He's such a generous person," I could hear one of them say. "Just so nice," another would say, shaking her head in shock and disbelief. The situation was hauntingly close to the very scene I prayed to avoid.

From the time we ventured out to begin this chapter of our lives, I knew we would need to trust God every step of the way. The news story provided a powerful reminder. I hungered to be in God's presence, as I knew our daily safety truly came from His provision. Mary's family was active in a local church, and they invited us to attend with them. But I already had other plans. I thought back to that time, not so long ago, when my popular hits radio station became a Christian radio station. Over time, the familiar voices with regular programs had become part of my commute. Now I lived within a few miles of the home church of Dr. Charles Stanley, one of the voices that had been such a valuable resource to me. Through his sermons on the radio, I had learned so much about God. Now, living such a short driving distance from his church, I knew we already had a new church home.

I vividly remember our first Sunday visit. Walking up the large stairs to the entrance, we were greeted by a booming voice and a smile. "Welcome to First Baptist Atlanta," the man said as he reached to shake my hand. We were welcomed with wonderfully warm, enthusiastic, southern hospitality.

Once inside, I was impressed by the size of the sanctuary. Without a doubt, it was the largest church I had ever seen. Scanning the church, we saw a large area for an orchestra and another for the vast choir. It was truly exciting to be there in person. As we made our way up the aisle, I was eager to sit near the front. The teaching of Dr. Stanley had already been a voice of hope for me, and a valuable lifeline. Now I was there to worship in his home church, spiritually very hungry, with my two children. Distracted by my enthusiasm, I almost forgot that Dr. Charles Stanley's broadcasts are telecast on national TV. Despite wanting to sit up front, we needed to choose seats out of range from the many cameras—a consideration I could not forget. It was but a reminder that life was different now. I needed to always be vigilant about my surroundings and conscious of any situation that could potentially jeopardize our safety and location. Here, in this church—a seeming refuge—the need for vigilance was no different.

"Let's sit over there," I said, pointing to a section well beyond the cameras. My children followed, yet unaware of the need for my careful consideration.

Once in our seats, the service soon began. Even at their young ages, Jennifer and Ryan came to enjoy Dr. Stanley's effortless delivery of a message each Sunday. We quickly adopted a great tradition after church: Waffle House. Just a block away from the church, it was so convenient. I found that while it is so easy to take for granted something as simple as a Waffle House breakfast, those are the very times in life to treasure. Together, as a family, we began to find our voice. We enjoyed lingering on a Sunday morning together, enjoying church, waffles, and most of all, each other.

CLEAR DIRECTION

It took only a few weeks to establish new routines. Mary was very generous with my children and me. Her support was incredible on every level, especially in answering our everyday needs. Previously, she had been afforded the opportunity to telecommute periodically. But she graciously sacrificed her basement office so that I could work from her home.

Church provided valuable spiritual nourishment, but I knew I needed additional support to deal with the effects of having been in an abusive marriage. With each day that passed, I gained new strength facing the realities of the situation we had left behind. I remembered the Web sites for domestic abuse that had been such a valuable resource in planning our escape. It seemed natural to turn back to those same sites to find local resources to help me now. After visiting Al-Anon back home, the idea of a support group for abuse seemed less foreign.

A women's resource center was located just a short drive from our new home. There, I found comfort with others who understood my challenges. In addition to hearing others share about similar pain, attending reminded me of why we had left. With time and distance, even with a situation like mine, it could have been easy to forget the depth of pain I'd endured. But the more I reminded myself of all I'd been through, the more I developed a resolve to move forward rather than look back. Regular participation in the women's group became a huge source of strength.

One Saturday I returned to the group, discouraged. My money had dwindled to the forty dollars in my wallet. Reflecting on a conversation I'd had with the private investigator before we left, I was keenly aware that certain actions would make it easier for Joe to find us. Something as simple as opening a bank account with a local address could put us at greater risk. Now, living in a new city with no bank of my own, I hadn't been successful finding a bank to cash my paycheck. None of the banks I had visited during the prior two weeks were willing to help and my company's California based bank offered no local branches. Without a local address or an account with their bank, they were unable to cash my check. *How am I going to continue to support us with my cash supply dwindling fast?* I wondered. *Mary has been so generous, but I don't want to rely on her. What am I going to do? How will I support myself and my children?* My mind raced as I settled into a chair in the meeting room.

The leader of the women's group spoke, interrupting my thoughts, "Good afternoon, everyone. Does anyone want to start?"

A woman sitting next to me, Amy, cleared her throat. "I would," she said. Although she was fairly new to the group, she participated that day out of sheer desperation. Her abusive husband had gambled away their money. She was in the midst of losing her home and her car, while her utilities were already scheduled for disconnection. She admitted that while she tried to squirrel money away, he had found most of it and used it to support his drug habit. Now desperate, she feared for her safety. The last few dollars she had managed to tuck away gave her just enough money to buy diapers for her baby and food for her children. She had come to the meeting with nothing left.

While she continued to tell the group about her situation, I heard God's soft whisper in my heart, *After the meeting, give her twenty dollars.*

My reaction was immediate: *I can't! I only have forty dollars myself!*

But then, I heard the voice a second time. There was no misunderstanding, as it was unmistakably clear. I knew I needed to comply. An hour later, as the meeting concluded, I quietly slipped twenty dollars into Amy's hand. She was visibly reluctant to accept the money at first, knowing my situation. But as the women of the group crowded around to give Amy hugs of support, I told her God wanted her to have it and left.

Moments later in the parking lot, I heard someone call my name as I unlocked my car. It was Amy, walking toward me, her eyes filled with tears of gratitude. "How could you have known?" she asked, as she pulled out a small amber prescription bottle from her purse. Her voice cracked as she said, "I took the last one yesterday." She paused to collect herself before she continued. "I'm a medication-dependent diabetic. I need this medication every day. I had no idea what I was going to do." She pointed to the refill cost printed on the label as a large tear rolled down her cheek. The cost clearly printed on the label: twenty dollars.

At that moment I was filled with a remarkable sense of renewed hope and peace. With a smile on my face and in my heart, I said with profound confidence, "Amy, I had absolutely no idea that you needed the money; God did. And while life looks impossible right now, He knew you needed this twenty dollars today. He knows what you need tomorrow. And, He knows exactly what you need the day after that."

Amy wiped a tear from her cheek as I continued to talk to her, both of us amazed by the moment that had unfolded before us.

"He alone can meet your every need," I said. "He alone can help you navigate every step on this difficult journey, helping you move forward one step at a time." While I spoke those words of hope to Amy, I realized they were the very words I needed to hear too. Fighting off additional tears, we hugged each other and said good-bye.

Encouraged by what I had just witnessed, I decided to visit one more bank on my way home. Despite the rejection I had received by all of the other banks, I felt optimistic. With my check in one hand and hope in the other, I entered a bank near the women's center. Moments later, with no questions asked, the bank cashed my paycheck.

Awed by all that had just transpired, I returned home. While I knew there would be challenges ahead, my newfound hope inspired me. I never saw Amy again after that Saturday; I have continued to pray for her and rest confidently in the knowledge that God is still looking out for her by meeting her daily needs, just as He has been meeting the needs of my family and me.

A few more weeks passed, allowing us to settle into our new home. I continued to work from Mary's basement in the suburbs. With a roof over our heads and my continued employment, we were safe. Despite living a life that was essentially underground, the challenges were relatively few.

One issue cropped up a few weeks into our new routines. That week, my children and I were introduced to the oppressive summer heat of the south. Unfortunately my van's air-conditioning system was no match for Atlanta's unforgiving July sun. After a few days of struggling to work, the air conditioner failed completely. Initially I thought we might be able to survive without fixing it. It didn't take long before the extreme southern heat forced me to reconsider.

Finding a local car dealer to assess my van took little effort. When I arrived, the mechanic greeted me. "Mornin', ma'am. How can I help you?" he asked with perhaps the heaviest southern drawl I had ever heard.

"I called earlier to have my van's air conditioning looked at," I said.

"Oh yes, I have your ticket right here, ma'am. Looks like you've got yourself a common one. We've seen tons of these. Lucky for you, it's covered by your warranty, ma'am." He looked up with a proud grin. "Oh, it'd cost you a few hundred otherwise."

Perfect, I thought and then realized what the implications of using my warranty might be. I had hoped to have my car serviced anonymously. I realized that I could not do that if I were to utilize the warranty. On the other hand, if I paid for the repair, I would need to pay by credit card, which I feared doing, knowing Joe could easily discover it.

I hadn't thought a situation as simple and commonplace as this, a simple trip to a mechanic, could undo months of planning to remain hidden. But with the oppressive southern heat beating down, something had to be done. I decided it was safer to use the warranty. A warranty repair record stays within the same company. A credit card, on the other hand, would be processed through the car manufacture and the bank, twice the exposure. Signing the paper to repair my van, I realized I had adopted a new thought process; looking at simple transactions would most definitely never be the same.

But it wasn't just simple repairs or church visits that caused me to look at my world differently now. The most commonplace thing, the simplest sound of a phone ringing, could set my heart racing because I knew it could be Joe. From the time we left, it had never been my intent to prevent Joe from being a dad to his children. My goal was to do what I could or whatever was necessary to ensure that he could be a dad without putting them or me in harms way. Before leaving, my attorney reminded me of the importance of letting Joe maintain some contact with our children. So, with great apprehension, I facilitated phone conversations between them. Joe already knew my cell phone number and, during that time, location wasn't easily discerned when calling a cell phone.

On any given evening our quiet routine could be disturbed.

"Susan, it's Joe. Put the kids on," Joe would say in a curt tone.

I'd hand the phone to whichever of my children was closer or whoever felt more like talking.

"Hi, Daddy," Jennifer said in her sweet voice.

"Hi, pumpkin, it's daddy. How was your day today?"

Being all too familiar with Joe's manipulative ways, I never was far away when my children were on the phone with him. Typically their conversations were brief, just simple check-in calls. Other times, I could hear in Joe's tone and words that he had been drinking.

"I don't think this is a good time to talk," I'd say.

But Joe didn't easily accept my boundary. "You can't deny me from talking to my own children, Susan!" Joe would shout.

That was never my intent, but he didn't see it from my perspective. From the beginning I wanted my children to have a dad, a wonderful, warm, present, sober dad. But from those very first brief conversations, my children picked up on the tension Joe brought to our world even from a distance.

"I don't want to talk," they'd say sometimes when he called. It was heart-wrenching. I empathized with my children—knowing they needed boundaries with their own father—and with Joe, who felt his relationship with them slipping away. Still, I did what I could to facilitate the occasional conversations, though never forcing my children beyond what they were comfortable with. While the issue of dealing with the calls from Joe or the repairs to my van seemed like monumental problems, it was nothing like the situation that was lurking just days away.

A few days after I had my van repaired, I was in the basement finishing up some work when my cell phone rang. It was my attorney back home. "Susan," he said, "the court has set an emergency hearing date. They want to meet to discuss an emergency custody agreement that has been filed."

Already? I thought. We were just getting settled into our new lives. My heart was heavy. I had known this day would come, but I wasn't ready for it just yet. Returning home would mean facing the very dangers that we'd run from. Returning would risk my life and potentially risk the safety of my children. Not returning had an equally tremendous risk: It would mean I would most likely lose legal custody of my children. Then if caught, I could go to jail. The options weren't appealing. I stood at a crossroads, torn between what was legally right and what was safe. Few people knew the details of my life and truly understood the dangers. In my moment of choice, I turned to the women at the resource center. Their response was resoundingly unanimous: Run. Create a new identity, run, and never look back.

In confidence, they spoke compassionately to me. One woman spoke of a contact she could give me to help us run, seek new identities, and assume new lives underground. "You need to go home and figure out what you want your new name to be. Then come up with new names for your children." *Run*, echoed in my mind. *Run*. If I didn't return home, what would my future be? Would I have to spend the rest of my life looking over my shoulder? Would I ever be able to see my family again? If I returned, would I ever really be safe? I had so many questions, yet no solid answers. I prayed, asking God for answers. I wanted clarity for the direction I should choose.

What should I do? I cried out to God. I knew I needed to trust Him for direction, but what now? With my prayer's *amen* my mind only raced faster. *I need a new name. But what?*

I picked up my Bible and began flipping through the pages. In doing so, I was reminded of the wonderful sermon I had heard months earlier when Cherie and I went to hear Dr. Stanley speak. Remembering the picture he painted of Daniel in the lions' den, who focused not on the lions but on God, was inspiring. With that thought, I opened to a passage in Daniel and began to read: "Daniel answered, 'May the king live forever! My God sent his angel, and he shut the mouths of the lions. They have not hurt me, because I was found innocent in his sight. Nor have I ever done any wrong before you, Your Majesty.' The king was overjoyed and gave orders to lift Daniel out of the den. And when Daniel was lifted from the den, no wound was found on him, because he had trusted in his God" (Daniel 6:21–23). Those words spoke to me. It was amazing to think God protected Daniel, even in a lions' den. It was also incredible to realize the strength of Daniel's faith. Faced with a life-threatening situation, he didn't waver but trusted fully in God.

I decided in dealing with my challenges, I wanted my character to resemble Daniel's. When confronted with compromise, Daniel stood fast in his faith. *Even when it risked his very life*, I thought. But, because of God's faithfulness to Daniel, he was unharmed. It was clear to me: I needed Daniel's courage. If I needed a new name, I decided I wanted my name to be Danielle. Now I needed a last name.

Flipping through the pages of my Bible, I was quickly reminded of all of the names that are changed in its pages. Jacob's name was changed to Israel in Genesis. Simon's name was changed to Peter in John. And Levi's name was changed to Matthew in the Gospels. Matthew. Something about Matthew resonated with me. *Matthew is the first book of the New Testament*, I thought. I needed a fresh start. I pondered. If I needed a new last name, it should be Matthews. Danielle Matthews. I had my new name.

I spent much of that night in prayer. *God, is this who You want me to be? Is this what You want me to do? Should I return? Should I run? Whose advice do I trust?*

In the early morning hours, in the still of the night, God answered my prayer. In my heart of hearts I knew the advice to trust was His. *Return*, He said to my heart. *Return. If you run, I will never be able to use your story to help others. Only if you return will you one day be able to share your story with others.*

God's words were remarkably clear. I knew without any doubt I needed to return.

THE ROAD HOME

Returning to our hometown brought an incredible array of emotions. While I knew it would be exciting to see my parents, I was keenly aware that returning would also mean facing Joe. My mind revisited statistics of how many women die after they leave. Based on what I knew, our return would need to be planned as strategically as our original exit. First and foremost, I wanted to ensure the safety of my children. In order to protect them, I knew they could travel only some of this journey with me. While I would have never considered leaving them behind in the South, I didn't want to take them back to our old hometown. There were simply too many potential dangers. Instead, I planned for us to fly to an airport about two hours away from home. There we would connect with my parents, who would stay at a hotel with Jennifer and Ryan, entertaining them, while I anxiously ventured to my court appearance.

Before we ventured north, I explained to Jennifer and Ryan that I needed to travel back to Maryland so that Joe and I could sort some things out. Aware of some of the dangers, though not fully aware how serious, they both were concerned that I would be safe traveling to our hometown.

I hugged them, reassuring them. "Mommy and Daddy are going to sit down with a judge who will help us figure things out," I explained, so that they might be reassured that I wasn't meeting Joe alone. I hated thinking that they didn't really have access to their dad. It certainly wasn't what I wished for them. In their own quiet ways, they reassured me that they understood. They didn't press for additional answers, nor did they ask to join me.

Our flight itinerary that day required two short flights with a brief layover and a change of planes. Knowing the size of the destination airport, I anxiously anticipated the small propeller plane necessary for the second leg of our trip. As much as I may have in any other situation focused nervously on the plane's incredibly small size, on this trip, that anxiety was surpassed by the airport in the middle of our journey. Our flight connected at the airport closest to where Joe and I had lived. It was the same airport I had used for my past business trips—trips that had generated so much relational stress. Unable to find another route to our desired destination, I now walked the familiar gates consumed with anxious thoughts. I did not want to linger on the concourse, and desperately wanted to board our second flight as soon as possible. I prayed we could pass through the familiar halls without a chance encounter with anyone we knew. It was the only time in my life I've been thankful to board a small propeller plane. After a short, bumpy ride, the plane's wheels touched down on the tarmac at our destination airport. My eyes welled with tears as I fought to keep my emotions at bay. Entering the door to the airport, we craned our necks. "Do you see them?" I asked as Jennifer and Ryan stretched, trying to peer past the gate.

"There they are!" Jennifer squealed. "Nana! Poppop!" she called, waving toward my parents on the other side of the partition just ahead of us. No words can ever describe the hugs that awaited us, such warm embraces full with love.

Just a few months earlier we'd said good-bye, truly not knowing when or if we might see each other again. Our good-bye had been a segue to the weeks of uncertainty both for my parents and for us. My mother's surgery and recovery had been an overwhelming success. Despite the promised threats against them, they were safe. They were equally thrilled at our arrival, safe and sound. Standing in the middle of a small airport, embracing my parents with my children, will remain one of the most indelible memories of my life. Unfortunately, we could not remain in that moment—after all, court awaited me.

We left the airport, the kids anxious to go to the hotel with their grandparents, while I had to get my rental car and head on to court. I hugged Jennifer and Ryan and told them I loved them before getting into my rental car. I held one hand to my car window with the sign language "I love you," and then pulled out of the parking lot and continued on my journey alone.

The two-hour car ride went by quickly. With each mile that passed, my struggle to let go of my building anxiety became even more challenging. *Lord, give me strength and peace,* I prayed, knowing I was driving directly into battle.

Although my attorney and I had planned to meet before court so he could let me know what to expect, it was the unexpected that I feared most. I knew he had been through this process many times before. While I was confident in his expertise, it was Joe I feared.

Our brief meeting before court brought no surprises. My attorney reviewed the emergency request for custody that Joe's attorney had filed. Additionally, he reviewed the stack of documentation we had that supported the actions I had taken to secure safety for myself as well as my children. When we concluded, armed with a yellow legal pad and a bursting accordion folder, my attorney and I ventured across the street to the courthouse. We were vigilant, knowing Joe too would soon be arriving and would be anticipating my arrival. Our arrival was incident free, enabling us to shift our focus to the hearing.

In the courthouse, one large area was dedicated solely to family court issues. A printed listing on a board identified which cases would be held in each courtroom. It wasn't until reading our names on the list that we learned who our judge would be and the courtroom assignment. Much to my dismay, the judge presiding over our hearing was rumored to have a bias toward fathers. Still, I tried to remain optimistic, knowing we had carefully documented my claims. Surely the judge would take into consideration all we had brought and remain fair.

Although it felt like an eternity, a short time later our case was called. My entire body instantly went numb as we entered a medium-sized courtroom with several wooden benches lining the back of the room. Two wooden tables were positioned facing the judge's stand, and Joe and his attorney had just taken their seats at one of the tables. My heart raced when I saw him. Settling into my chair, I felt uneasy. Months of emotions seem to well up in me and turned in my stomach. Before I could calm the butterflies, we were instructed to rise for the judge's entrance.

The judge looked down at the court documents before him. His job that day was not to determine our long-term solution but instead rule on what needed to occur in the interim while we waited for our full hearing. As the judge reviewed the paperwork, he asked questions of Joe and his attorney, as well as of me and my attorney. His questions seemed methodical while he focused on a variety of aspects of our case.

Then, with little warning, the judge looked at me and demanded I disclose to the court where I was currently staying. I looked at my attorney. "I can't," I mouthed.

My attorney challenged the judge, requesting I not be required to answer the question. The judge looked at me again, and with a pause, he asked me once again to tell the court where I had been living. After taking such careful steps to leave safely, I was fearful for not only my safety, but for the safety of Mary and her family. She had so graciously taken me in. Now I was being asked to disclose her address and identity. I was paralyzed with fear.

My attorney redirected, and a conversation between the judge and the two attorneys ensued. Following their conversation, the judge moved on and didn't continue to press for my location. He, however, ruled that visitation needed to begin within the next few weeks. Additionally, I would be required to live within a reasonable distance from Joe to facilitate visitation between Joe and our children. Lastly, the judge ordered that our initial visitation be supervised, perhaps the only consolation he gave in consideration of all we had brought forth. A schedule would be established as soon as I could relocate back to Maryland.

Stunned, I looked at my attorney. *What just happened?* I thought. With the judge's decision, my world was about to turn upside down.

Convinced Joe was the only victim in the courtroom that day, the judge ordered me to move back to the area so Joe could begin to have regular visitation with Jennifer and Ryan. With a cold, steely, author-itative voice, he condemned "women like me" who in his opinion try to use the system to keep fathers from their children. The judge discounted any of our documented proof, including the folder full of notes from my private investigator. He was only willing to yield to one request: supervised visitation. It was a small victory that seemed more of a consolation prize. I knew our battle was long from over, as the order that day was only temporary. Before we left, they gave us a date for our full hearing. It became obvious that our court battle would be a marathon rather than a sprint. My mind raced, but with the firm tap of the gavel, I had no time to be lost in my thoughts. My dramatic exit was about to unfold.

As my attorney and I stepped out of the courtroom, I was met by a waiting man. Knowing the very real danger I would face as I left the courthouse that day, my private investigator had carefully planned my exit. The man immediately whisked me through a door that led to an emergency exit stairway. We went down a flight or two of stairs before he led me through another doorway. His indirect path led us to a floor of the parking garage, where a car waited. The man opened the back-seat door for me and instructed me to lie on the floor. He hopped into the front seat and the car sped out of the parking garage. The man in the passenger seat scanned the sidewalks and road around us, seeking to ensure our clean getaway. A block from the courthouse, we were joined by our first follow car, a surveillance car charged with the task of ensuring that no one else followed us. Each turn, each road change was monitored by the second car. About five minutes later, my driver pulled over. There, another car waited for me. When it was deemed the coast was clear, I switched vehicles, and the process continued. Just as in the first car, I stayed on the floor of the backseat while my new driver and surveillance car took me to an undisclosed location in a nearby town. We had arranged that I would retrieve my rental car there before my drive to my hotel rendezvous with my parents and children. Straight out of a dramatic suspense movie, it was a remarkably exciting exit.

Once behind the steering wheel of my rental car, the adrenaline rush that had accompanied my courthouse departure quickly faded. During my two-hour drive back to the hotel that day, I continually asked God, "Why?" Though I remembered that He said I would one day share my story, facing the reality of moving home now shook me to the core. With continued doubts, I asked God where He was. "I thought You were going to protect me," I challenged. I didn't understand why we needed to move back, nor could I begin to make sense of our court appearance.

With the distraction of the day's events replaying in my mind, my drive passed quickly. I was greeted by my parents with hugs and tear-swollen eyes. They shared my same doubts and fears. Before moving forward, we decided to take the next day as a minivacation. Despite the many challenges ahead, for one day we put everything on hold to fully pursue laughter and fun at a local amusement park. It was a park my family had visited when I was growing up; now I could share it with Jennifer and Ryan. With beaming smiles, they slid down the slide of the Old Woman in the Shoe's house, from the top of her giant shoe to the ground. They waved and laughed as they steered old-fashioned cars around a curvy track. Despite the rain that rolled in during the afternoon, dampness could not darken our spirits. It was a day full of cherished memories.

The next day brought a whirlwind tour of apartment complexes, as one of my sisters and I searched to find a new home for the three of us. With a court deadline, I needed to quickly find something. Moving back to my familiar stomping grounds did give me the advantage of knowing which areas might be affordable on my new single-income budget. Other than cost, my list of requirements for our new home was a short one. I wanted a building with a lock on the building's front door and I wanted to be above the second floor. Concerned about our safety first, I felt any other amenity was a bonus. Wherever we moved, I knew it would quickly become home because we'd be there together.

After a day of visiting three or four different complexes, we found an apartment that was perfect for my children and me. Our fourth-floor, two-bedroom apartment was just across the parking lot from the local elementary school, a perfect benefit for a newly single mom. We moved in just a week later, but not before our long journey to Georgia and back with my van full of our belongings. My mom agreed to make the long, emotional trek with us. Due to pressing time constraints for us to be back in Maryland, we planned to make the trip in a short one-to-two-day window, beginning with the first morning flight to Atlanta.

Though sleepy when we arrived, my mother was eager to thank the wonderful woman who had kept her daughter and grandchildren safe. It comforted her to see where we had been and where we had called home. It didn't take long to pull our belongings together and pack the van. We graciously thanked Mary and her family for everything they had done for us. But no words seemed adequate to convey our sincere appreciation for how Mary had provided a safe place for us when we had nowhere else to go. We gave final hugs all around and then climbed into the car to head to our new home. The driving portion of our journey began.

Although our trip north was full of uncertainty about the future, it was comforting to have my mom along for the ride. The hours in the car gave us valuable time together, free from the normal distractions. The much-appreciated time was a gift after everything we had been through since our visit in June. Although we knew it would be difficult to complete our trek in one day, we planned to drive as far as possible before giving in to exhaustion. We watched mile markers and road signs to encourage us to press on; however, the road we traveled that day seemed to offer remarkably few road signs through the Carolinas. We eagerly hoped for some indication of our progress, but were disappointed as abysmally few were to be had.

Out of necessity, the lack of signs became a source of humor. Otherwise, it would have easily become a source of incredible frustration. Of the many things we could remember from that day, we still laugh about our unsuccessful search for highway signs to give us hope. Regardless, we made it as far north as northern Virginia that day. Pleased with our day's progress, we found a comfortable hotel to rest our weary heads. In the morning, we completed our trip and arrived at our new apartment with our belongings. We were home.

In the busy days ahead, our family of three celebrated Ryan's fifth birthday just prior to the start of a new school year. Enrolled in the school just across the parking lot, Ryan and Jennifer began kindergarten and first grade in our new community. As the year began, new, fun opportunities for them to be involved in surfaced. Jennifer began taking baton-twirling classes with a group after school. Ryan began

T-ball with a group of children his age, each with a mitt that seemed to be half as big as their bodies and helmets that consumed their small heads. It was a joy to watch them have fun and occasionally pick clover in the field when they lost focus.

It didn't take long before it was time for my dreaded return to court. My first appearance had left me understandably doubting the judge. I wondered if it was possible for him to be just or fair in our case. I was frustrated that because of his experience, as well as because of others who have falsely claimed abuse, it was harder for those of us who were truly dealing with abuse. I also understood the dangers of my situation in a way that he didn't seem to, and I knew he had not really heard what we had to say. Entering the court, I hoped this second time would be different. By now, perhaps he'd had time to consider the magnitude of my situation.

My attorney and I entered the familiar hearing room. The same wooden table and chairs awaited us. "All rise," a court worker said in a booming voice.

When the judge entered, a swell of anxiety rushed over me. I prayed he would hear the facts and understand the very real danger I faced. He wasted no time getting to business. "Are you and your children now back in the area?" the judge asked.

"Yes," I replied.

"Please tell the court your new address," the judge demanded.

With a sense of déjà vu, I looked at my attorney and mouthed the words, "I can't." *Has he not read our documents? Does he know nothing about my situation?* I thought, my heart pounding.

"Please tell the court your new address," the judge repeated.

"Could we have a few minutes?" my attorney asked.

Much to my surprise, the judge provided us the opportunity. I was disheartened that this was how our hearing started. I thought it was bad enough that this same judge requested the location of where we'd fled to. Now he was asking where we currently resided. I still feared for my safety and had no desire to say my address out loud in court.

After a few minutes, the focus returned to the judge, now ready to proceed. Before my attorney could speak, Joe's attorney cut him off. "Your honor," she began "we do not find it necessary for her to reveal her current address. As long as it is documented by her counsel, we are satisfied."

I was shocked. It seemed very unlike Joe to provide such a consideration given his anger both before and since I'd left. While I didn't understand his motivation, I was grateful the judge didn't press further, and once again, the need to disclose our address passed.

Before the judge established a new visitation schedule, he announced his first order. He demanded I acquire our dog, Alley, back from the family who had adopted her. Without hesitation, he continued with his rulings; the schedule would provide supervised visits once a week initially with the cost of the supervisor split between Joe and me. Once supervision was no longer required, our children would begin the split life between Joe's home and mine. Each Wednesday night would afford Joe the opportunity to spend dinner with our children. In addition, they would spend every other weekend together.

Only when you navigate the treacherous waters of divorce can you understand the depth of the lose-lose situation. As a spouse broken by the devastation, you suffer a tremendous loss. Greater still than the brokenness of a divorce is the pain you suffer as a parent watching your children be torn between two parents and two homes. In order to support my children best through the emotional challenges of navigating between two homes, I vowed to never use them as message carriers. If a message needed to be given to Joe, I would use e-mail, not my children. If they had a prized possession they wanted to take to Joe's house, even if I had given it to them, I would let them choose. Giving them the right to manage their own belongings would give them something they could control in a time when most of their lives seemed helplessly out of control.

ENDURANCE

Our new fourth-floor apartment was just the right size for our little family of three. We had what we needed. The kitchen had just enough space for the small table and chairs I found on sale at Kmart. I took the smaller of the two bedrooms, giving my children the large master bedroom with a giant walk-in closet. That provided each of them room to have their own space with more than enough room for their toys and clothes.

Adapting to our new home was one of the easier transitions we needed to make. Adjusting to other changes required much more energy. Probably the biggest adjustment to life as a single parent was realizing just how little downtime I had. From the time I woke up in the morning until the time my head hit the pillow at night, I was on. If I wasn't working, I was parenting. And, even though I technically got a break once my children went to bed each night, I was still on, always responsible. Truly, the concept of downtime became nonexistent.

Soon after we moved back, the court-ordered supervised visitation began. Never having been exposed to anything like that before, I had no idea what to expect. In fact, the concept of divorce and visitation was foreign to me. We were advised that there were two types of supervision possible. We could elect to have Joe visit our children in a community-run center with a supervisor or the supervisor could travel to his home. Both cost the same. Considering which would feel more natural to our children, we chose the latter of the two options. The court worked with us to find an individual willing to provide the service and then split the expensive cost between us. The venture added hundreds of dollars to both my and Joe's monthly budget—an additional expense, that while necessary, proved challenging.

When Jennifer and Ryan began seeing Joe, I was glad to have a third party manage the transfer. Initially I dealt with the supervisor to set up meeting places and times. She, in turn, dealt with Joe. For the first several months, I met her in the local McDonald's parking lot and she drove my children the short distance to their dad's house. Their two-hour visit concluded the way it had started with the supervisor driving them back to McDonalds to meet me. During their visit, I found ways to keep busy in and around Joe's town. My new apartment was about a half hour away, making it impractical to head home while Jennifer and Ryan visited him. Instead, I planned trips to the grocery store or found other ways to keep busy.

In the beginning, the visits went well for the most part. Jennifer and Ryan assumed that the supervisor was a friend of their dad's helping him out, a perception that seemed a bit more palatable than the thought of the woman being a paid court-ordered participant. During those initial visits, Joe avoided alcohol. In fact, after the court appearance that had initiated the visitation, Joe later admitted that he quit cold turkey. The bold move on his part temporarily yielded a far more stable Joe—after he lived through intense withdrawal that could have killed him.

Looking back, I don't recall how long sober Joe lasted. In the court paperwork, Joe was barred from consuming alcohol while he was responsible for our children. Perhaps that served as a deterrent in the beginning. Regardless, we still encountered bumps in the road with visitation. At times my children just didn't want to go. "Do we have to go?" they'd whine. "I don't want to," one would say. I was torn whenever they resisted. I didn't want to force them to go, but at the same time I realized we had a court order in place. I knew if they didn't go, Joe would waste no time contacting the court to tell them I was uncooperative.

Joe picked up on the fact that his pint-sized visitors were not always thrilled to spend time with him. Each time he detected the resistance, I braced myself for an endless barrage of phone calls that always followed. "This is all your fault!" he would shout, accusing me of "poisoning" our children against him. "You caused this. What did you tell them?"

When I sensed a troubled Joe, I did my best to let many of his calls roll to voice mail. I purposefully turned the volume down on the answering machine so that Jennifer and Ryan couldn't hear the rantings of their dad as he routinely recorded his outrage on our machine. As much as I may have wanted, unfortunately I couldn't ignore all of his phone calls. In court, I had been warned not to impede Joe's access to our children and was told that he needed to be able to contact them via phone between visits. I quickly found that one way to assess Joe's state of mind was the distance between his phone calls. Some days he seemed to spiral out of control, calling more than a dozen times in quick succession. Some calls were just seconds apart, other times he'd wait up to five minutes before calling again. Occasionally on those days, the repetition wore down my nerves to the point that I just wanted the madness to stop. In a lapse of better judgment, I would answer hoping once and for all the harassment would end. Each of those times I was instantly reminded why I had ignored those calls every other time. Without fail, those conversations always yielded the most intense arguments with Joe. Between berating me for being an awful mother, and accusing me of turning his own children against him, Joe was not at a loss for harsh words. Many times, those calls did not have the most civil ending. Instead, after I had heard enough, and realized that a rational two-way conversation was not possible, I simply said, "Good-bye, Joe," and hung up. Unfortunately, the one thing Joe hated more than having his calls ignored was being hung up on. When I hung up on him, the cycle of rapid-fire phone calls began once again. Other than time, the horribly vicious cycle could only be stopped by one thing, turning the phone off.

I did what I could to encourage my children to look forward to the time they spent with their dad. Despite the headaches he would often give me, I truly felt that they needed a good healthy relationship with their dad. As long as I felt they were safe, I saw the visits as a potential for them to rebuild their relationship. Even with my attempt at a positive attitude, it broke my heart to tell them they needed to visit when they so desperately wanted to stay with me. One Saturday, Ryan was adamant that he did not want to go. After arriving at our typical McDonalds rendezvous with the supervisor, he made his opinion clearly known. "I don't want to go," he said loudly, pouting and crossing his arms.

"You need to go, honey," I said, trying to sound encouraging. "Your dad's looking forward to seeing you."

Standing at the door on his side of the car, I encouraged him to hop out. He looked up. "I don't want to go," he said again even louder this time. The supervisor glanced at me, looking extremely annoyed. She could see that I was trying, however, she was less than amused by the situation. When Ryan finally inched out of the backseat of my car and slipped into her car, with one swift motion, she reached over and slapped him. I was horrified! What supervisor slaps a young child? My mind raced. *What can I do? What legally can I do?* She was a court-appointed supervisor with a schedule that offered no flexibility. I wasn't prepared for a situation like this. I had no frame of reference on how the court would handle my refusing the visit. The judge had proven he was less than sympathetic to my situation. *What will he do if he hears I refused a visit?* With the conflict in my head still swirling, the supervisor shut the door of her car and left with my two children. I was truly numb, paralyzed by fear and sadness. It was the longest two-hour wait I have ever endured.

First thing Monday morning, I contacted my attorney with my concerns. That morning we swiftly fired the supervisor; the court appointed a new supervisor to work with us until supervised visitation was no longer needed. I shared my fears about going against the court order with my attorney. He reassured me that should there ever be a situation when I needed to go against the court, I should use my good judgment. I knew I would never again allow a court order to prevent me from making a right decision for my children. Fortunately, I was never in a situation like that again.

GOD OF THE IMPOSSIBLE

Settling into life as a single mom had its own share of challenges. There never seemed to be enough time, energy, or money left at the end of the day. I looked forward to the start of the school year because Jennifer would be in school for the full day, Ryan for half. It would provide some relief to my challenge of balancing work and taking care of my children full time. A new routine would provide some welcome structure. Still, more than anything, I felt I needed more time with my children. Spending time together provided us the security we were hungry for. We needed to find a new normal to help us begin to heal.

But I also had to afford this new life. I began looking for ways we could save, ways to make my money go further. I decided my minivan was a luxury that I could no longer afford, which made it necessary to trade down to a car offered on a special sale-priced lease. Despite making what changes I could think of to reduce our expenses, the changes just weren't enough. Caught between a rock and a hard place, I knew that if I worked more, Jennifer and Ryan would need to be in day care more, which would cost more, which would ultimately defeat the purpose. I found myself wanting more time with them but needing more money to afford life. Something needed to change, but what?

Not seeing how it could work, I felt desperate. Armed with two Scriptures that gave me hope, "Take delight in the Lord, and he will give you the desires of your heart" (Psalm 37:4) and "You do not have because you do not ask God" (James 4:2), I prayed, *God, I don't know how, but I need more time with my children, and I need more money to get by. Please help me.* I remember my simple prayer as though it were yesterday. It was one of the most open-ended short prayers I have prayed in my life. Such an odd little prayer. I'm not sure what I expected God to do with it. But I trusted Him fully with the needs of my heart and the provisions for my family.

A few days later, I bumped into a coworker from several years earlier on the sidewalk outside my office.

"What are you doing these days?" he asked.

We took a few moments to update each other on our departments and projects at work. Then, before we went our separate ways, he said, "I'm not sure if you'd be interested, but I have a peer out in California who's looking for someone with your background."

The out-of-the-blue job opportunity sounded intriguing. Over the coming days, I had the chance to exchange messages with the hiring manager. He just happened to be flying from Europe back to California via the airport near where I lived. We planned an airport interview for a few days later. Our meeting went remarkably well, our conversation effortless. His team spanned from Belgium to California to Singapore. The team's need seemed to be a perfect match for my background. It not only sounded exciting, it was an opportunity to work from home.

Through our conversation, I learned that because the team was so dispersed, my work hours did not need to follow traditional hours. I could essentially pick my own hours. What an unexpected answer to my odd little prayer. The position, while a lateral move in my company, would prove to be financially rewarding because I could shift my workday to earlier in the day. When Jennifer and Ryan finished school, my workday would already be complete. Financial relief came by reducing my dependency on child care.

In one sidewalk encounter, God had orchestrated the answer to my request: more time with my children and financial relief. It was far more than I could have ever expected. It was yet another reminder of God's abundant faithfulness. It also proved to be a wonderful reminder to me to not put parameters on answers to prayer. Out of the desires of my heart I reached out to Him. His answer was far beyond anything I could have dreamed or even imagined was possible.

During that same time, the radio station that had been such a positive influence in my life before we moved became a source for new inspiration. I stumbled upon a radio broadcast from a church in a nearby town. After listening to several broadcasts, I decided to visit one Sunday. The welcome we received reminded me of our experiences at First Baptist Atlanta. While there was no Waffle House next door, attending this new church quickly became part of our weekly routine. Within a few weeks, we began attending the Wednesday night service in addition to Sunday service. The midweek service provided just the boost we needed to help us get through the rest of the week. I found the extra reminders of my source of strength, peace, and protection invaluable.

* * *

As I anticipated, the start of the school year brought welcome new routines to our new little family of three. Each weekday, my workday started while Jennifer and Ryan still slept. I planned a work break to have breakfast and walk to school with them. A few minutes before the start of the school day, we ventured across the parking lot to their adjacent elementary school.

My priority became ensuring that Jennifer and Ryan were safe, healthy, and happy. I poured my energy into providing everything a mother could possibly give. We had the basics—an apartment to live in, a car to get us where we needed to go, and a church we called our spiritual home.

One afternoon on our walk home from school, Ryan looked up to me with a worried look. "I fell today," he said.

"Are you okay?" I asked.

"Yes," he replied. "I just fell."

In my mind, I discounted the situation. After all, he was a busy five-year-old boy. I told myself there was a logical explanation.

Two days passed before another report. "Mom, I fell again today." Again he wasn't hurt, although concern was visible across his young face. Something about this second incident stirred my mother's instinct. I didn't understand what had happened, but my concern began to grow.

That evening, Jennifer and I sat playing on the living room floor. Ryan, planning to join us, started across the room. Suddenly, without warning, he was on the ground. He looked directly at me and said, "Mommy, that's how I fell at school."

My mind raced. What I had just witnessed was not normal. It was obvious that Ryan's legs literally gave out without warning. I knew we needed to find answers.

Late the next afternoon, we visited our pediatrician's office. Regularly listed in publications as being one of the best pediatricians in the area, I was sure our doctor could help us find answers. At the completion of the exam, instead of answers, he handed me two slips of paper, one a referral to a specialist, the other an order for blood work. Before heading home, we stopped briefly by the blood lab downstairs for the technician to complete Ryan's lab work.

Once home, I scheduled an appointment with the specialist. Luckily, the first opening was only a week out, not too bad for a specialist. A few days later the phone rang, breaking my focus on my work project.

"Hello, this is Dr. Williams. I'm calling with the results of Ryan's lab work."

I was a bit surprised to hear the doctor's voice on the other end of the phone. My heart instantly sank while my mind raced. *What did they find?* Typically it is rarely good news when the doctor himself calls. Concerned, I feared this time would be no different. He continued, explaining that the blood work came back with a positive result indicating muscle deterioration. He encouraged us to follow up with our specialist appointment.

A few days later, we arrived at the specialist's office for Ryan's appointment. After filling out a clipboard full of paperwork, we sat down for a brief wait. Soon Ryan's name was called. A nurse ushered us into an examining room and let us know that the doctor would be with us momentarily. She invited Ryan to sit up on the paper-covered examining table. "Hello," the doctor said extending her hand to shake first Ryan's hand and then mine. "Let's see what we have here, shall we?" she said to Ryan. "Ryan, point, flex; okay, point again," the specialist instructed as she examined Ryan's feet and legs. She had him complete several exercises, including walking so that she could see how he functioned.

She looked down over her notes before speaking. "I'd like to complete some additional blood work," she began. "I would like to check Ryan for Charcot-Marie-Tooth disease, or CMT as it's often called."

What? I thought. I had never heard of that disease.

The doctor continued, explaining that it is a degenerative disease. The remarkably high arches that Ryan and I share can be one of the more obvious symptoms. Recently Ryan's gait had changed, with tightening Achilles tendons; he walked mostly on his toes.

"These types of muscle degenerative diseases are not reversible or curable," she said. She gave us a sheet with exercises for Ryan to complete at home while we waited for the conclusive lab results. Exercise and therapy to aid his flexibility and to work his muscles would provide short-term help while we waited for the diagnosis. The genetic testing, we were told, could take up to six weeks for results to be returned.

Over the coming weeks, Ryan fell often. On more than one morning, he complained that his legs were too weak and tired for the short walk to school. On those days, I reached down and picked him up, giving him a piggyback ride to school. Although I worried, I prayed for him and tried to find a way to stay positive. The more I read about his suspected disease, the more my heart grieved. Still, we attended his appointments and he continued his exercises.

Four long weeks into our wait for results, I received an unexpected phone call. A nurse from the lab called to inform me that Ryan's blood had been drawn into the wrong type of test tube, and the test could not be completed with the blood that had already been drawn. Disappointed, we waited once again after a new visit to the lab.

I knew that while I eagerly waited for Ryan's diagnosis, putting a name to what he was going through didn't matter to him. As a child, he only knew he had good days and bad days. On a good day, Ryan could go the entire day without falling once. Those were wonderful days. On other days, he fell often. In fact, with his falling, he began getting bruises on his legs. I felt completely helpless to protect my young son.

One Sunday morning, Ryan cheerfully bounced into his kindergarten Sunday school class. There was such a wonderful group of teachers and children in his class. Our church family provided us a warm environment where we were welcomed and felt we belonged. Near the end of the class, a teacher asked the children if any of them had any prayer needs.

Ryan's hand quickly shot up. "Can you pray that I stop falling and that my bruises go away?" he asked. In his innocent faith-filled heart, he knew where to look for help.

Remarkably, Ryan never fell again after that Sunday morning. From the heartfelt request of a child to the ears of an almighty God, Ryan's prayer was heard.

A week later, I received another phone call from the lab. The woman on the other end of the phone explained that the diagnostic lab had inadvertently lost Ryan's blood work. Profusely apologetic, they couldn't confirm his diagnosis. It comes as no surprise; no further testing was ever required. After a positive test result for muscle deterioration, and after weeks of falling and countless bruises, Ryan was cured from a disease that is neither curable nor reversible.

In the months that followed, I found myself clinging to the incredible string of answered prayers we had witnessed, truly awestruck by

God's provisions and faithfulness. Amazed by one incredible answer to prayer after another, I seemed to have a front row seat to witnessing God's remarkable ability to solve the impossible. With each incredible step, I found reminder after reminder that with God so much more was possible than I could ever have imagined. In the time from that fateful December day when Joe told me that I would never get away from him, God had provided a safe exit; my nosey neighbor couldn't get through to his cell phone while I left. Out of nowhere, Mary offered us a place to stay. And since our return, a big answered prayer was my amazing new job, which had reduced my child care need while providing for me and my children.

While I clung tightly to all the wonderful answers to prayer, I found myself holding on to fears and challenges. Adjusting to life as a new single mom was exhausting. *When will life be normal again?* I wondered. *Will I ever have enough energy, money, or time at the end of any week?* I doubted it. The little downtime I had came only as a result of visitation, which came with its own incredible amount of stress. Joe routinely called to harass me and tell me that I was an awful mother and person. Some mornings when I awoke, it was as though I stepped out of bed into a cloud of pain and hurt that seemed to linger. I longed for the energy and time to get through everything that life demanded of me. But somehow my prayers for relief didn't seem to yield any quick answers. Unbeknownst to me, I had begun to follow a predictable pattern. In prayer, I pleaded to God for relief. Yet when my prayer was done, I picked up my pile of grief once again, carrying my burdens as I went on to face the world. I longed for new answers to my prayers, yet I felt I was stuck with reminders of past answers rather than new ones.

One morning, frustrated and feeling stuck, I asked God for insight. There in quiet prayer reflection, God explained, *In one hand you are holding tightly to blessings you've already received, like your wonderful new job. In the other hand, you are gripping your hurts. You ask Me to bless you more and take the hurts from you, yet your hands remain clenched shut with a firm grip. Your hands are not free to receive. I will not pry your hands open; you must first let go.*

I looked down at my hands and curled my fingers closed. He was right. Figuratively my hands were full. Not wanting to let go closed my heart and closed me off from receiving anything new from God. I turned my hands over and uncurled my fingers. *Please, help me to let go,* I prayed.

DEFINING MY IDENTITY

My new job afforded me wonderful flexibility while providing us with enough money to get by. I was tremendously thankful for the ability to be more present with my children and to eliminate the need for expensive day care. Although my position provided so many obvious benefits, it also came with a few unexpected challenges. One such challenge was the direct result of my new team's being a truly global team. Even though I had previously been a member of a geographically dispersed team when I worked with Mary, the majority of that team was located in Atlanta. I and a few others simply worked as remote team members. My new team brought "geographically dispersed" to an entirely new level. Now my peers worked in Belgium, Singapore, California, and a host of other places. No one location hosted a core group of team members. As a result, my manager conducted weekly teleconferences and began quarterly in-person meetings. To make travel "fair," he decided that each team meeting would shift to a different location and would be hosted by the resident team member. The opportunity to see the world sounded fabulous; however, I was unsure how I could manage even infrequent travel as a single mom. Because the job offered the much-needed daily flexibility that enabled me to be a full-time mom, I knew I needed to find a working solution.

Thankfully my parents offered to stay with Jennifer and Ryan when I needed to travel. When their time permitted, they both came. Other times, my dad couldn't break away, so my mother came alone. Together, they quickly learned my children's likes, dislikes, and daily routines. Jennifer and Ryan's close relationship with my parents made their visits special. Excitedly, they showed my parents where their school was and proudly introduced them to their teachers. Without a doubt, Jennifer and Ryan loved having their grandparents visit. The only downside to these visits was how much they hated it when I was gone. With all we had been through, the three of us had grown very close; to my children, my presence had become synonymous with safety and stability. To ease my absence, I often found creative ways to help them track how many days until my return. Sometimes I created a calendar for them. Other times I picked up trinkets at the dollar store and wrapped them. Each day they would open one trinket until I returned. Each evening when we spoke, they excitedly shared what they had opened that day. While it didn't totally make up for my being away, it often proved to be a good distraction.

My favorite trip while I was part of that diverse global team was a fabulous trip to Brussels. Despite the long working days, the lovely scenery gave me a minivacation, a respite from all of the stresses at home. Our beautiful hotel was just a few short blocks from the picturesque town square lined with cafes, bakeries, pubs, and shops. Each day, the cobblestone streets bustled with activity. The alluring aromas from the bakeries wafted through the streets, tempting us daily to indulge in the local fare. Perhaps the greatest temptation lining the nearby streets were the chocolatiers that offered decadent Belgian chocolates. Truly, one of the greatest benefits of the trip despite the long working hours was the extremely valuable and desperately need-ed downtime. For the few nights I was there, when I wasn't working, I treasured the quiet moments and the valuable refreshment it offered. My trip also included the wonderful highlight of a visit by Natalie, one of our former au pairs. Since I was was just a short train ride from her home, Natalie took the opportunity to come visit me while I was in Belgium. I welcomed the reconnection, as it provided some additional healing after all I had been through. We enjoyed dinner together when my schedule allowed and spent an evening exploring Brussels together.

While spending time with a familiar face from my past allowed me to fully be myself, I found myself to be a bit more guarded around my new team. My bubbly, personable team members shared a lot about their families. Each time the group got together, I learned more about each one of them. Over time, it genuinely felt as though I knew them the way you might get to know the person who sits just one cubicle away in a traditional office setting. I knew their children's names, their spouses' names, their favorite vacations spots, and family hobbies. It was interesting and fun to get to see into the lives of my collection of coworkers from all over the world.

Overall, the position was a wonderful fit. I enjoyed the implemen-tation project that kept me busy each day while I enjoyed the people as well. With the project's overwhelming success, I naturally expected only a glowing review from my manager. I had grown accustomed to positive reviews and strong rankings each year since Joe had taught me how to speak up all those years ago. Perhaps that's why I was shocked to get a dose of firmly constructive feedback from my manager. He began the review by praising my hard work and solid work ethic. Then, after a pause, came the more challenging feedback. My manager proceeded to explain that with a fully geographically dispersed team, the team's identity and core came from the strengths of the connections built among the members. After assessing the team growth, he did not feel as though I had brought enough of *me* to the team. Regardless of how well I *knew* my team members, I had remained aloof and they didn't really know me.

I thanked him for his honest feedback. As I reflected upon what he had shared, I realized that I had become less trusting, more withdrawn, and far more likely to listen than to speak. Perhaps sharing any part of myself at that point in my life just didn't feel possible. I didn't yet know who I was in the wake of the devastating collapse of my marriage. As far as interests or hobbies, I needed to figure that out once again. My highest priority had become my children. Beyond that, I hoped for a safe, peaceful life, not the sort of thing you blurt out to a group of coworkers while you are trying to get to know them. Without question, I realized that God had given me incredible strength and protection that had gotten us this far. My faith was growing, creating a new solid foundation for me and my children. My life's focus had shifted to exploring who God wanted me to be and being the parent that He called me to be. But, it still wasn't something I knew how to share with my team. How surprised would my old manager be if he realized why I was so quiet? Certainly the feedback gave me food for thought. I knew it wouldn't be appropriate to share many of the details of my life, but I realized that I needed to continue to work to find my voice. I also needed to start to exercise the muscle of building relationships. During the time I was married to Joe, I had let so many slip away. Now I needed to begin building new healthy friendships and relationships.

I never expected a review at work to prompt soul-searching on who I was, what interested me, or even how I would share any of that with the world around me. But it did. *Who am I?* I was a single mom, mother of two, pulling myself up by my bootstraps, desperately wanting a "normal" life. I had become a firm believer that trust is earned, not freely given. No, I hadn't opened up to my new coworkers, but I'm not so sure that is surprising given everything I had been through. Being transparent truly wasn't something I welcomed at that point in my journey. My wounds were simply too fresh. For years I had worked to gain what looked like the American Dream. The façade I maintained back then would have been easier to share with my team than my current reality.

Outside of seeking "normal," I needed to figure out who I was before I could begin to share it effectively. As I began to reflect, I began seeing qualities developing in myself that I hadn't recognized before: I had become determined and resilient. Those qualities, combined with my faith, became a valuable source of daily strength. I welcomed those qualities. My reflection, however, also took me back to my high school days as I sought to understand how I ended up married to someone like Joe. I tried to understand how I could have ignored all of the red flags that had surfaced over the many months leading up to this juncture. With such a loving family, how did I end up with such low self-esteem that I thought being with Joe was better than being alone, and that somehow I wasn't good enough for anyone else? I began to realize that

I had allowed opinions of a few unkind people to distort my opinion of myself, undermining my sense of self-worth.

One such person was Neil. Neil was a tall, cute, popular football player. My freshman year he was a junior. But more important, he was the on-again-off-again boyfriend to one of my sisters. My high school had somewhat of an unwritten rule that upperclassmen didn't typically talk to freshman. But Neil talked to me. Sure, it was because of my sister, but nonetheless, he talked to me. In the beginning, he was friendly. Typically he asked if I had seen my sister or asked about something pertaining to her. One day Neil ran into me as I was walking into the German room.

"You're taking German?" he asked.

"Yes," I answered, heading into my class. Both he and my sister were in an advanced conversational German class and the German club together. For some reason, that was the day Neil's attention toward me began to shift. The next time I bumped into him, he laughed. *"Du bist eine deutsche Ente!"*

I looked at him, puzzled.

"You'll have to go look that up," he said, knowing that my beginner-level German probably wouldn't understand what he meant.

He was right, I didn't. Later, looking up the translation, my heart sank. Neil wasn't being fun, kind, or cute; he was being cruel. "You're a German duck!" He had laughed at me. In one hurtful remark, Neil had honed in on one of my insecurities. My extremely high arches caused my feet to turn outward. It was one of the things that made me different. In high school, it is far more desirable to blend in than to be different. Despite having custom-made orthotics to support my arches, there was nothing I could do; my feet naturally turned outward.

Popular Neil had found a way to take his cruel insult to a new level by always saying it in German. Walking down the locker-lined halls of my high school, it didn't matter whether he was walking past me or was halfway down the hall, he shouted, "Du bist eine deutsche Ente!"

If I had the misfortune of walking with a friend or classmate, without fail, they would ask what it meant, adding insult to injury. For the two years my high school existence overlapped with Neil's, I was subjected to frequent ridicule. His on-again-off-again relationship with my sister made it hard to avoid him, because he shared the insult no matter where he saw me, even at our home. As an insecure ninth grader, just wanting to fit in, I had no idea how Neil's repetitive insults were steadily tearing down my self-worth.

Unfortunately, Neil wasn't my only challenge in high school. During the same time that he began his insults, I was actively working to perfect my basketball game. I was far from a natural athlete, but still I loved basketball. Not happy with my performance on the junior varsity team my freshman year, I decided to devote time in the summer to improving my game. I was determined that sophomore year would be an even better year. My sister Liz and I shared the same goal. Together, we decided to participate in a few back-to-back basketball summer camp programs. The intense sessions provided drills, games, and focused training sessions from the time they woke us up in the morning until we collapsed into bed at night. When we arrived at the last camp, we were quickly separated into different groups based on our skill level; my group was not the level I had hoped for. Rather than be discouraged, the placement fueled my desire to succeed even more. I dug deep, applying myself like never before. On the final day of camp, I was filled with immense pride; I had managed to win the one-on-one tournament for my age group. With camp coming to a close, we filed into the bleachers for the closing remarks. The camp director and coaches stood before a trophy-lined table. One by one, they called out the names of individuals who had won awards. With each name they called, my smile grew bigger because I knew it was just a matter of time before my name would be called. When they finally called my name, I proudly stepped down from the bleachers accepting my one-on-one championship trophy. My hard work and dedication had finally paid off. Back in the bleachers, I sat, still focusing on my trophy. I was shocked to hear my name again. "And, lastly, we have the trophy for the most improved. The most improved player goes to…" me! It went to me! Beyond excited, I was thrilled to leave camp with a trophy in each hand. I couldn't wait to get back to high school to tell my coach. No doubt, it was about to be an awesome year.

Just a few weeks later brought the start of my sophomore year. I eagerly anticipated basketball tryouts. I just *knew* this was my season. As a necessary formality of playing sports, I visited our family doctor for signoff on my heath forms. I wasn't expecting anything out of the ordinary, but I was wrong.

"Your murmur sounds different from the last time you were here," the doctor explained to my mother and me. "I'd like you to get it checked out by a specialist before I sign off on your papers."

No worries, I thought. *I've heard of other people with heart murmurs before. I've never heard of it being anything other than something people grow out of. I'll go to the specialist and continue on as planned.* A week later, after a few tests, my mother and I sat across from the cardiologist. "You have bicuspid aortic stenosis," the doctor said. His words meant nothing to me. Soon I'd know exactly what he was talking about. He went on to explain that my aortic valve was not formed correctly. Not only was the opening smaller than it should be, but it would continue to get tighter and tighter, eventually requiring open-heart surgery. Before I could understand how it would impact my life, he carefully laid it out before us. My new diagnosis meant that I needed to give up playing the French horn in the band. He explained that the pressure of playing would not be good for my heart valve. I had started playing five years earlier while I was still in elementary school. While I knew that would be difficult, I was entirely unprepared for what the doctor had to say next.

"I'm sorry, but I cannot clear you to play basketball," he said, looking compassionately at me. My heart fell in an instant. In my head I screamed, *But I was the one-on-one champion. I won the most improved award. What do you mean I can't play basketball!* I was crushed.

But, even as an awkward high school sophomore whose life has just been shattered, step by step, I began to put my world back together. In the coming weeks, I took up the xylophone so that I could remain in band and not lose contact with my friends. Almost instinctively, I realized that while I could no longer play basketball, I could remain active with the team by becoming a statistician. Slowly, with time, I began finding new hobbies that the cardiologist allowed, such as tennis and horseback riding. My world had shattered, but somehow resilience persisted. I began to redefine myself.

Now, so many years later as I reflected on high school, I could choose which situation I would tap into to help define myself. I could choose to be minimized by the Neils or the Joes of the world, or I could be the resilient individual who refused to remain crushed when her world shatters. The choice was obvious; I knew I needed to trust God for strength to tap into the latter.

CHARACTER BUILDING

When our divorce agreement was finally processed, it seemed like we had been going through the exhausting battle for an eternity. At the recommendation of our attorneys, we worked out the division of every ounce of our lives together before returning to court. The seemingly endless process was a painful back and forth. I didn't care to fight about furniture, possessions, or even money. I cared most about the custody of our children. Extremely concerned over the stability of their father and his alcoholism, I fought for primary custody. In the end, on paper the court would call our arrangement joint custody; however, I had the ability to make decisions when we could not agree on something, regardless of the topic. While returning to Maryland was a loss in our divorce battle, the fact that I gained the ability to make decisions for my children was a huge victory.

Perhaps the greatest surprise in our agreement was the order that after two years, I would gain possession of our family home and our beloved dog, Alley. The two-year agreement was our unique compromise. Joe didn't want to move right then, but he said he did not want the house long- term. I, on the other hand, did not want to move back too soon because I wanted to wait to assess if returning in the future could be safe. The delay allowed Joe to continue living in the home for the foreseeable future while giving me the necessary time as well.

When the time finally came to move back to our family home, it felt right. Pulling into my old driveway on that sunny summer Saturday brought a rush of emotions. It felt surreal. Walking up the sidewalk, the kids running ahead of me into the house, I could almost feel the stare of the same neighbor who had so intently watched me move out and alerted Joe. *I wonder what she and my other neighbors think of me now*, I thought. *They know only Joe's side of the story and are loyal to him. I can only imagine how intensely they must judge me*. Still wrestling with how to overcome their negative opinions of me, I followed my children into the house. I felt as though they had tried and convicted me of a crime without even considering my side. I wanted them to like me. I didn't want to be thought of as a cruel and heartless person. Conflicted about how to resolve the situation, I wanted to defend my character and shout out, "I am not the horrible person you think I am!" I was at a loss. *Lord, can I ever change their opinion of me?* I prayed.

The answer I got wasn't at all what I expected; it was complex because it meant doing nothing to directly change my neighbors' opinions. Instead, the answer guided me. *Live your life in such a way that they will see your character and understand your integrity by who you are, not by what you or others say you are*, the words of His spirit gently guided my soul.

"Really, God?" I asked. "How can I do nothing about it?"

His wisdom that followed was remarkably liberating. *If you try to change their opinions, your focus will become their opinions, rather than what matters most. Live a life filled with good character and they will either see who you really are and change their opinions or they won't. Your worth is not and never will be determined by what they think.*

With those words still resonating in my mind, I was freed on the very day we moved in from the judgmental opinions of my unknowing neighbors. Sure, over the following days as we settled into our home once again, I challenged the thought of not defending my honor a few times. But each time was a short-lived internal conversation ending with a reminder to put their opinions in perspective and reminding me of where my focus needed to stay. Pondering my newfound wisdom reminded me of how I had been influenced by the words and opinions of others in my life; Joe and Neil both came to mind. How liberating it was to realize that I no longer needed to be burdened by their opinions or critical thoughts.

One night, sitting in the living room after putting the kids to bed, I opened my Bible. There, in front of me, was another reminder to keep my focus directly on God instead of anything else: "Finally, brothers and sisters, whatever is true, whatever is noble, whatever is right, whatever is pure, whatever is lovely, whatever is admirable—if anything is excellent or praiseworthy—think about such things. Whatever you have learned or received or heard from me, or seen in me—put it into practice. And the God of peace will be with you" (Philippians 4:8–9).

In the months that followed, I slowly began getting reacquainted with many of our neighbors. Probably the first and easiest to reconnect with were our next-door neighbors, Dave and Eileen. Dave, a big hunter, had three meticulously trained chocolate Labradors. If Alley was out in our yard while Dave's dogs were out, the dogs all congregated at the fence as if they were visiting. Other times they ran the length of the yards together watching each other through the chain-link fence. The dogs found a way to play together, despite being in separate spaces.

Over the years, Alley had established a relationship with Dave, a dog lover through and through. He fussed over her and often joked that when she was done visiting us, she needed to head home, pointing to his house. It was wonderful to have a neutral topic such as dogs to discuss. We weren't forced into awkward personal conversations, nor did they ask prying questions. Instead, we allowed casual over-the-fence conversations about dogs to pave the way.

I can't help but think that as parents themselves, they noticed how I poured my time and energy into my children. With hunched-over back-breaking effort, I taught them to ride their bikes on the street in front of our house. I played catch and had batting practice in our backyard. We played for endless hours on the swing set, the one Joe and I had so carefully picked out together. We even planted a garden—a very, very tiny garden in our yard—together. No doubt, over time they could see that I was the same Susan they had met years earlier. I still shared the same parenting values and love for dogs.

In time the surface "Hi, how's it going" over the fence became "How are you really doing?" They also started looking out for us. On many occasions, Dave mowed our front yard before I could get to it, such a kind gesture. Despite Dave's assistance with mowing and his great friendship with Alley, I had far more conversations with Eileen. She had noticed that when we originally left, Joe and Sarah were away together. Without needing to ask many questions, she put some of the pieces together. She had also noticed the frequency of Sarah's visits after we left. Although she didn't know my entire outrageous story, she knew enough. One day she said, "You know, Joe told many of the neighbors that you drained your bank accounts before you left."

"I'm not surprised," I said, knowing that Joe had used that complaint against me in court as well as included it in rants left as early voice mail messages. "I think he told that to anyone who would listen."

"Yes, I think he did," Eileen said.

"I'm sure he forgot to mention that I paid all of our bills that were coming due before I left, including the mortgage," I said, not at all surprised that he had twisted the truth to appear as though I had taken our money and run. In reality, I didn't take any of our joint account money with me and instead made sure he wouldn't be blindsided by bills. In the months leading up to our departure, I had squirreled away some of my own income and only took that money.

Eileen nodded. "Your hydrangeas have really taken off this year," she said, almost as if she simply wanted to clear the air by acknowledging what Joe had told her. She didn't seek an explanation or share extensively. Rather, that conversation proved to be a transition. Instead of being the ex-wife of her former neighbor, I became her neighbor anew that day.

Over the years, my focus has remained on putting what I have learned from God into practice in raising my children, in doing the best I could for them while following where God has led. It shouldn't be a surprise that in addition to Dave and Eileen, my other neighbors' opinions about me changed over time. In fact, all of our neighbors' opinions changed except for one: the neighbor who watched us flee from behind her curtain. Despite her inability to see the truth, I have been freed from a life focused on looking at my value or self-worth through the eyes of others. That neighbor may never understand the truth nor know my true character, and I doubt she will ever know all that happened in the house across her quiet suburban street. But I know it is not my responsibility to change that.

Despite concern about judgmental neighbors, settling into our old home occurred with greater ease than I expected. Like putting on an old pair of shoes, even with all that had occurred, it was comfortable. Our furnishings were simple, but somehow that was okay. Through my children, our family quickly made connections with other families in the neighborhood who had children the same age. The start of the school year had also brought new routines and friends into our lives. Jennifer and Ryan adapted well to their new elementary school as well as to the school bus routine.

Although life continued to settle into a new normal, I was often reminded that although I was now divorced from Joe, he would remain in my life because of our children. Just as in the early years of our marriage, time could stretch out with mostly positive interactions. During those times, Joe worked with me to coordinate visitation. We were flexible with holiday arrangements, making it possible for Jennifer and Ryan to see both of us on an actual holiday. Much like the Joe I had first met, when times were good, Joe was easygoing and generous to work with. Times like those built my hope that he could become the father I wanted my children to have.

Despite our ability to occasionally work together, we still had our fair share of conflict. Many of our challenges came during times that Joe slipped back into manipulative patterns, which typically coincided with his alcohol consumption. Much like the cycle of abuse I had become familiar with, now, from a distance, I could watch Joe cycle. During those times his kindhearted calls to check in with our children were often accompanied by accusatory harsh phone calls attacking me. An almost predictable pattern emerged with Joe's behavior. My children seemed to have gained a sixth sense, avoiding visits with their dad when he became challenging. More than once, I temporarily gained hope that Joe had changed, really changed. But each time, over and over, he proved that he was still the same Joe.

Regardless of how kind or cruel Joe could be, in the years since our divorce, I no longer felt threatened by him. I think at some point in time, he stopped being dependent upon me. With greater distance, I could see that we had an unhealthy codependent relationship. The longer we were apart, the more Joe no longer depended on me, and I no longer fed that old unhealthy dependence. I no longer tried to fix him and no longer enabled his behavior to have the same influence over my life. As Joe pressed on in his own life, he continued his relationship with Sarah. Emotionally, he increasingly depended upon her for his stability, which ironically provided greater peace for me.

One of the ongoing greatest sources of issues between Joe and me was Joe's inability to adopt the court's ruling. Despite the requirement that each of us attend a parenting program designed to raise awareness of the impact of divorce on children, Joe never attended. Instead, he became possessive of Jennifer and Ryan's belongings and often challenged them if they wanted to take something from his house to our home. While it hurt my heart to see those challenges, it broke my heart more to see their faces at school events or baseball games as they scanned the audience looking for their dad. Despite knowing about the events, he typically chose not to participate. I desperately wanted my children to have a father, even if he was no longer fit to be my husband.

FAMILY IN FOCUS

During this time adapting to our new life, I found myself inspired by hopeful memories uncovered through soul-searching. Warm memories from my childhood reminded me of the foundation my family had given me. However, it yielded an obvious reality; somewhere along the line, my life had become nothing I had hoped it would be. I never set out to be a divorced single mother. All those years ago, when I naively took a chance on a relationship with the one person who was ever present and vowed loyalty, the one thing I wanted most was not to be alone. In hindsight, being alone would have been so much simpler. Now, I juggled work and full-time parenting. "Me time" became non-existent. My focus was on pouring myself into my children in hopes that I could protect their hearts with my love.

I wanted a family like my own had been. Why was it so elusive? While I'm sure my parents encountered obstacles in life of which I was never aware, we had a beautiful home in a quiet neighborhood filled with the loving support of both a mom and a dad. My parents made both parenting and marriage look deceptively simple. The home I had grown up in had previously been my paternal grandparent's house before they passed away. It was filled with family history, and the love that was passed down through the generations. The love my grandparents and parents filled that home with lingered throughout the big old farmhouse.

My parents were both active in and supportive of our interests and activities. No matter what my sisters or I were involved in, they were there for each one of us. Whether Mom and Dad were in the bleachers on a brisk fall Friday night cheering on the marching band or sitting on a blanket at a softball game, they were fully present. My mom's natural leadership came through in her volunteering with Girl Scouts. My dad, right there to support her and us, also volunteered. I vividly remember countless other special times we spent together, from painting classes at a local art shop to wonderful lunches and teas, including the annual mother-daughter banquets at our family's church. We were never surprised when my mom won a door prize for being the proud mom of the most daughters. Although I didn't see it then, there was such a sweet innocence in those times that I now cherish. Mom's smile consumed her whole being as she introduced us to others. We knew she loved us and was so proud of each one of us.

I also remember wonderfully warm memories with my dad, a proud Rotarian with a heart as big as Texas. Around my dad, I always felt loved and accepted. He shared his hobby of fishing with us, teaching my sisters and me to fish at a young age. I'll be honest though; I always let him put the worm on the hook and take the fish off. We also enjoyed many great meals at local restaurants together. One place, the Fence, was a family favorite. It sat right on the banks of our local river and had a wonderful scenic view. It was known for the best seafood, brought right to your car or the picnic tables that overlooked the river. Of all our favorite times with Dad, one we looked forward to every year was the Christmas celebration at Dad's Rotary Club for the members' children. That night was always a special time with Dad, complete with a delicious meal and a special appearance from Santa Claus. When I close my eyes I can still see the large banquet room, an overwhelming vision of wood that reminds me of an oversized hunting lodge. Plaques and flags were proudly displayed on the wall, conveying the mission and accomplishments of the organization. Although the venue in itself was a bit drab, the joy and love that filled the room made it a remarkable place.

Where will those memories be for my children? I wondered. *Can they ever really have the same sense of family with ours shattered beyond repair?*

Society had a name for families like ours: "broken." I had no frame of reference for how this could work. The few single-parent families I knew seemed to struggle, not the word I wanted at the foundation of the legacy I hoped to leave for my children. I didn't want them to grow up one day and reflect back on discord, challenges, or struggles. Instead, I wanted their memories to be filled with warmth, love, and family—the way my memories are. How would that ever be possible now? Navigating this new life, I kept discovering that things were so very different now. I didn't have to look far to find reminders.

One that took me by surprise came by way of my children's elementary school. The start of a new school year brought a swarm of energetic volunteering moms, each eager to find opportunities to be part of the daily school routine. They descended on the school with vigor at the beginning of the academic year. Soon it became very clear that in my affluent suburb, many of the moms either worked part-time or were solely stay-at-home moms. Excitedly, they signed up for the many opportunities to help, blessed with the flexible schedules necessary to serve the school in whatever capacity they desired.

My heart sank. While I was absolutely thrilled to have a job that could get our family of three from one day to the next, I knew that I would never be able to participate at the school to the extent of the other moms. Quickly, they learned the names of all of the children in their child's class. They gained an in with many of the teachers, being such a valued resource in and around the classroom. They formed connections with one another and seemed to have a mom alliance. Most of all, they had the cherished opportunity to participate in their children's education beyond my own means.

Across the board, my children had wonderful nurturing teach-ers with open communication, just like the teachers I still remember from my own elementary days. Unfortunately there was one major exception, Mrs. Miller, Ryan's second-grade teacher. At the first par-ents' night, the parents were ushered into the classroom, each invited to sit at their child's desk. A few of the volunteering moms darted to their children's seats almost as though the music had quickly ended after an impromptu round of musical chairs. Proudly they found their spot while the rest of the parents navigated the classroom, appearing a bit lost. Once I found Ryan's desk, I pulled out the miniature chair. Feeling a bit like I had been transported to the Land of Oz full of munchkin-sized furniture, I sat down, bumping my knees on the tiny desk. As I soaked in the projects around the room and looked through the papers in Ryan's desk, Mrs. Miller welcomed the enthusiastic parents, assuring us of the wonderful year ahead. I have to admit, I didn't get a warm, fuzzy first impression. She just didn't seem to have the same level of instant warmth that my children's other elementary teachers had. Still, I tried to remain optimistic that it would be another great school year.

A few weeks later, I welcomed the opportunity for my first parent-teacher conference with Mrs. Miller. The preceding weeks leading up to conference had been a bit challenging, with more than one note sent home informing me that Ryan had been disruptive during class. I looked forward to discussing her observations rather than having to rely on back-and-forth notes. It wasn't until that meeting that I truly saw a different side to Mrs. Miller. As the conversation began, I wasn't prepared for what this apparently very judgmental, very opinionated teacher would say next. As she began to address what she deemed as disruptive behavior, she said, "Coming from a home like yours…" her words trailing off in my mind. *A home like mine?* Truly I was stunned by the audacity of a teacher who had no idea what we had been through and now condemned our small family. *A home like mine?* I replayed. A million thoughts raced through my mind with a million different responses to her judgmental statement. As though I were a deer caught in headlights, I was paralyzed, not able to form even one of my million thoughts into an appropriate response. Instead, I carefully listened to every thing she shared, making a permanent mental note of her prejudice.

On the short drive home, I replayed our conversation over and over, offering countless responses, some more appropriate than others. Although I couldn't change the past conversation, I knew that how she had acted was completely unacceptable. The next morning I contacted the school office and asked them to switch Ryan to the other class for his grade. His small school unfortunately offered just two classes per grade level. Understandably, based on the condescending attitude his teacher had displayed, I was concerned that her class would not be the best learning environment for my son. After a conversation with the principal, I was disheartened by a resounding no. Informed that the class sizes were already out of balance, the school administrators were unwilling to make any class-assignment adjustments in Ryan's grade.

Notes home continued throughout the year. Mrs. Miller remained challenging on many levels. She was convinced that my son was one of the weaker students in her class academically, and taught him based on her perception. She assumed that his perceived acting out was based upon his inability to keep up with her pace. Her judgmental approach, however, yielded to my own sweet redemption when the school tested Ryan's class to identify gifted and talented students. I'm sure Mrs. Miller's opinionated thoughts were challenged when Ryan's scores squarely placed him in the gifted and talented range. I, on the other hand, was not at all surprised that a gifted student could come "from a home like ours."

Beyond the challenges at the school, I didn't have to look far for other reminders that life was different now. Everyday situations brought their own surprise reminders. Baseball was one such surprise. With Ryan's enthusiasm for baseball continuing to grow, he asked to sign up for both the spring and fall seasons of Little League. The seasons had distinct qualities that formed a predictable pattern. Team practices brought a handful of dads together to eagerly assist the coach, each dad taking on an area of interest such as batting practice, fielding, or assisting the pint-sized pitchers. On game days, the sidelines filled with families—grandparents, moms, dads, energetic siblings—all coming together to cheer on their respective players. The same handful of dads present at practice eagerly assisted the coach in often-vain attempts to bring order to the player's bench or to help the young players focus on the field.

I welcomed the routine, the sense of normal it brought to our lives. The twice-a-week games and practices in between made it necessary to plan out our week—the structure a welcome addition to our schedule. Those times were priceless, cherished times with both Jennifer and Ryan, but they still brought a painful reminder that my children didn't have the perfect family.

As visitations with Joe improved over the course of the year, Ryan invited him to his games. He too wanted his dad on the sidelines cheering him on, encouraging him. But Joe often instantly declined. Looking back, as sad as it was to see Ryan's long face as he hung up the phone following a somewhat predictable no, it was far less heartbreaking than the other scene that routinely played out. Occasionally Joe would answer, "I'd be happy to come to your game, son." Ryan's smile would grow with anticipation and excitement. On game day, dressed in his cute Little League uniform, Ryan would warm up with his team. Between taking his turn to throw or catch the ball, his eyes would scan the sidelines, first excitedly and then more anxiously as the start of the game approached. As his team took the field for the first inning, he would crane his neck to check the parking lot behind the field. Then his eyes would frantically scan the sidelines from one end to the other. The ritual was repeated many times until eventually the first batter stepped up to home plate. Ryan's heart seemed to visibly sink as he returned his focus to his game. For several innings the sad scene replayed itself, and with each, it appeared his young heart sank deeper, until eventually he stopped looking for his dad to arrive.

My heart broke each time I witnessed my son's heart-wrenching disappointment unfold. Powerless to influence a different outcome, I decided it was time for me to do something different instead. Despite the dad-dominated world of Little League, I began volunteering. I found a niche where I could help and be more active with the team; I learned how to manage a baseball scorebook. Eventually I became a fixture in the dugout, assisting with the batting order while logging the game's actions on the oversized charts in the scorebook. Although I know it didn't replace his dad's presence, I know Ryan felt more supported by my participation.

Beyond life on the baseball field or in the school classroom, perhaps the biggest change that came with single-parent life was the financial stress it brought. From my traded-in van to a TV that no longer had cable, I didn't have to open my checkbook to be reminded that there had been a huge financial impact to life as I knew it. While I did what I could to shield my children from the changes and sacrifices that were necessary to get by, I knew that, deep down, they understood that things were not what they once were.

If I doubted their awareness, proof came one Saturday afternoon with an innocent visit to the mall on a December day to see Santa. We waited eagerly with the other excited children and a few screaming infants who weren't so thrilled to be there. With each flash of the elf-dressed photographer's camera, the line inched closer until it was Ryan and Jennifer's turn. In line, they soaked in all the excitement Santa's village had to offer. Oversized, spectacular ornaments and glistening snowflakes hung high above from the ceiling, while on the ground an assortment of giant packages wrapped and decorated with fancy bows provided a place for a few giant teddy bears to sit. The large teddy bear in the middle moved his arm as if to wave at all of the waiting children. In the middle of the collection of decorations, a colossal Christmas tree near Santa stood tall above the other decorations almost as if it was stretching to reach the hanging ornaments. Two life-sized decorative soldiers marked the entrance to Santa's area. While we waited, Ryan and Jennifer's little necks craned to take in all of the sights, not wanting to miss even one ounce of the magic. Finally, we were at the front of the line, standing next to the soldiers with anticipation. The kids' eyes grew wide with excitement as the elf helper said, "Next." The two bounded with joy over to a very merry-looking Santa before scooting up onto his lap for a photo. Santa leaned toward each in turn, listening attentively to their Christmas lists. After they shared the wishes of their hearts, they looked up and smiled. With the flash of the camera, my children jumped down and darted over to me.

"What did you ask Santa for?" I asked.

Nothing could have prepared me for the innocent childlike answer that followed. "We asked Santa for a PlayStation," Ryan said with wonder in his eyes. Then after a brief pause, Jennifer added, "We know you don't have enough money for one and he does."

My smile grew wide. My heart warmed. While they hoped for something big, they understood the change that had swept through our family of three. I was touched that they never considered asking me for their big-ticket dream item. I knew at that moment exactly what would be under our tree Christmas morning. No matter what I needed to do without, or where I needed to trim our budget, I knew more than anything I wanted to give them a little childlike magic that year. Under our tree that year was one of their biggest Christmas surprises ever, wrapped up beautifully with a bow: a PlayStation from Santa. I didn't need my children to know the gift was from me. Instead, I wanted them to bask in that Christmas magic and perhaps restore even just a little bit of innocence to their young, sweet lives.

FREEDOM THROUGH FORGIVENESS

I loved being able to give such a magical gift to my children at Christmastime, allowing their young hearts to believe in the impossible. But I had no idea that I was about to receive my own amazing gift: the gift of freedom through forgiveness.

From the time I had begun to find my faith, journeying through my unraveling and broken marriage to living life as a single parent, I hadn't really ever considered forgiveness. It's not that I had pondered forgiving Joe and then made a conscious choice not to. Rather, it simply wasn't anything I'd even remotely entertained. That is, not until one morning's commute to work.

On a commute that started out like so many others, I turned on the radio to accompany me on my drive in to the office. The host and guest of that program were discussing the power of forgiveness. I'll be honest; I listened not because it was a topic that I thought I needed to understand. Rather, I just I found it interesting. That radio program turned out to be an appetizer. The main course followed just a few days later.

Digressing, I must say that sometimes that is just "so God." Have you ever noticed that there are times that a topic or Bible passage "falls" into your path at church, on the radio, or in some other way? You feel that twinge inside, as though you recognize that it is exactly what you needed to hear or read. If it isn't enough that you consciously realize the connection to where you are in life, the same topic will circle back in front of you again. It's as though God is saying, *In case you thought that was a coincidence, let Me remove any doubt.* I have had many such instances. The subject of forgiveness was one of those for me.

A few days after listening to the radio broadcast on forgiveness, God gave me an opportunity to really hear a message on forgiveness. Stubborn me heard the words of the radio program, but that discussion remained in my head instead of propelling me into the act of forgiveness. Now I realize it was God's intent to transplant those thoughts from my head to my heart.

Several weeks earlier, before listening to the radio discussion, I'd begun participating in a small group at our church called DivorceCare. It offers hope and support to those going through divorce. I didn't know very many people who had divorced, but of those I knew, too often the individuals seemed bitter and angry long after their divorce. Hoping to avoid their same fate, I signed up, not really knowing what to expect. After all the steps I had taken to break free from my relationship, I didn't want to remain trapped by the past. On this particular week, the DivorceCare topic was—you guessed it—forgiveness.

As the members of our group arrived, each took a seat in the circle. Within our few weeks of meeting, DivorceCare quickly became a highlight of my week. The group, about fifteen of us in all, were at different emotional places on the journey to dealing with the collapse of their marriages. Some individuals were still married but with little hope, and they sought out support in the event that divorce became inevitable. Others were already divorced but seeking healing from their wounds. As with other weeks, our group started with a video segment. The topic of forgiveness brought lively discussion to our small group. The host challenged us by stating that unforgiveness leads to bitterness. His message was simply that we each have a choice. We can forgive, or we can choose a life of bitterness.

It can't be a matter of choice—live with freedom or live with bitterness—can it? I thought. Who would consciously choose to live with bitterness? I had seen people who were angry and bitter for years. I knew I didn't want that. But still, I struggled. How could I possibly forgive a man who not only had had an affair but had had that affair in our home and with a family friend? He was emotionally abusive and had even planned my death. He had single-handedly brought immense pain and suffering into my life. How could I forgive him? The message left me challenged, making me realize that I needed to better understand forgiveness.

Not wanting to be condemned to a life of bitterness because of a choice I would make, I sought answers. DivorceCare provided numerous resources for additional reading. I picked a book they recommended, knowing I had to learn more.

Over the coming days, I began plowing through *I Should Forgive, But...* by Dr. Chuck Lynch. In the book, Dr. Lynch explores the excuses commonly used as reasons people do not forgive. *An interesting approach, as I certainly have a list of reasons not to forgive my ex,* I thought. In fact, if I interviewed the average person on the street, I'm sure I would hear, "You have a right to be angry." Or, "He should pay for what he did to you." Any number of seemingly appropriate or socially acceptable responses might follow. But I felt challenged not to seek popular opinion as a basis for my actions but to seek an understanding of God's Word on forgiveness. The two viewpoints, I've learned, can be vastly different.

I was amazed to learn that we are called to forgive, even when the other person isn't sorry. We are called to forgive when the other person doesn't even realize how he or she has hurt us. We are also called to forgive when we cannot forget what the other person has done.

As I struggled to really understand forgiveness, a visual analogy developed for me. I looked at forgiveness as though it were an invoice with payment due. In the world of business, companies track what is owed to them on invoices. If someone fails to pay their invoice, their debt could grow to include interest. As long as the debt is owed, it remains on the books so that it is not forgotten. Eventually, the unpaid debt would be turned over to a collection agency. In life, it is easy to live remembering all of the wrongs someone has inflicted on us as individuals. As time goes by, our anger can grow, adding to the pain, increasing the hurt. Much like a log of unpaid invoices, we carefully remember the injustices, hoping to one day receive justice or perhaps even revenge.

God says instead, "I will become your collection agency. I've already paid the ultimate price for the wrongs done to you by someone else. You no longer need to be burdened by carrying the list of wrongs forward in life with you." How freeing to know that He is the collection agency, not me.

I decided I would make an attempt to put this understanding of forgiveness into practice with my situation with Joe. I knew it wasn't possible for me to forgive him on my own, but I was ready to trust that God could help me through this. I took out a paper and began writing a comprehensive list of every way Joe had wronged me. Over the following days, I added to the list as I thought of items not yet written down. Seeing the growing list was helpful, as it illustrated my points of pain.

After several weeks of consideration, my list was complete. I thought of my example and reminded myself that the debt was not owed to me but to the One who had already paid for it. I prayed over the list and agreed to let God be the collection agency for the huge list of debts created by Joe's mountain of wrongs.

I didn't hear a clap of thunder; the sky didn't instantly part when I gave my list over to God. It wasn't an immediate, visible change. But over time, the result was far better than I could have ever expected. Over the next few weeks, my anger cleared like clouds after a storm. Joe still refused to admit his abuse or label his actions as an affair. And he most definitely was not considering the need to give an apology either.

The irony was, my turning over the list of wrongs to God didn't even involve Joe. It was my choice, between God and me. The peace it brought was transformational! I no longer carried the burden of all that had happened to me.

Too often in life, we try to remain the collection agency, hoping to fix injustices or staying obstinate because we perceive we are owed something by those who have wronged us. What we often fail to recognize is that the role consumes an incredible amount of energy and requires us to remember all that is owed. How else would we know that the debt has been paid in full? In reality, the debt isn't ours to collect. Instead, we need to forward the list to the best collection agency that exists, God. The move is incredibly freeing. And it allows us to stop spending our own valuable energy trying to right the wrong.

* * *

Perhaps one of the hardest aspects of divorce can be the loss of other relationships, such as other friends, neighbors, or extended family. People often feel compelled to choose one side over the other. Unfortunately, it only serves to add to the losses already experienced.

During the months and years following our divorce, our situation was no different. Balancing our new lives, I hoped to minimize additional losses for Jennifer and Ryan. Over time, I reached out to family friends as well as our previous au pairs. In the years that followed, nearly all of our former au pairs have had the opportunity to visit. Each visit reestablished a connection with someone I truly valued as an extension of my family, someone dear to my children. I had absolutely no desire to make them choose sides; I simply wanted them to still be family.

Rachel's visit was no different. She had been a close family friend before the divorce. She came over one afternoon after we'd moved back into our old home. We had a lovely visit, flipping through the pages of a large photo album, remembering a time years ago when Rachel lived near us. It was amazing to see how much my children had grown over the time. So much had happened since then; life was not as innocent as it once was. We looked through recent pictures, catching Rachel up on more current activities from school concerts to T-ball. We laughed. We reflected. Having her visit was a like a hug reaching out of the past, saying, *Yes, everything will be okay.*

When we finished looking at photos, Rachel slowly closed the cover of the album perched on her lap. She looked up and hesitated before she spoke. "I need to tell you something, and I'm not sure where to start." Her voice cracked as she spoke. She paused again. Then her words came out in a rush. Though I don't remember exactly what she said, the conversation went something like this. "Sarah wasn't Joe's only affair. I've really been struggling with guilt. He and I had a relationship when I lived near you. The first time we were together, I was going through a very tough time. He comforted me. I didn't want it to happen again. I felt so guilty after it happened the first time, but Joe told me that if I didn't, he would tell you. He said it would devastate you. He also said he would divorce you and take Jennifer and Ryan from you. I felt so trapped." She had only been eighteen when all of this transpired.

Rachel proceeded to explain how Joe had victimized her over a several-month period. Regularly, Joe propositioned her for sex. In return, he promised to stay quiet about their indiscretions. The manipulation she described was classic Joe. He had perfected the ability to know exactly what to say and how to say it to get people to do exactly what he wanted. He convinced Rachel that by staying quiet, she was causing me less pain than if I knew. He used his influence and her guilt to manipulate her.

Over the years since that time, she continued to be haunted by her experiences with Joe and her overwhelming guilt. She desperately longed to ask me for forgiveness. We talked for hours that day. She explained that she needed me to know the truth and no longer wanted Joe to hold the power of their secret over her. She asked if I could ever find it in my heart to forgive her. Her words, filled with pain, hung in the air. While she felt full of guilt, I knew better than anyone Joe's manipulative power. She had been a victim as well as a participant in her past. Both roles tormented her now.

I leaned over and gave Rachel a lingering hug. Forgiving her took little effort on my part. Scarred from her relationship with Joe, now as an adult, she needed to face that chapter of her life in order to heal and move on. And I wanted nothing more than her healing, knowing how freeing mine had been for me.

BLESSED

At my first meeting with my attorney all those years ago, he attempted to encourage me by saying that someday the drama would subside and we would settle into a new normal. I remember wanting to laugh; in fact, I think I actually did. I truly thought that would never be possible. But with time, Joe's primary focus shifted away from me, giving way for my children and me to enjoy wonderfully normal routines. On weekday mornings, with a familiar screech, the school bus stopped like clockwork at the end of the driveway. Like clockwork the kids returned home again in the afternoon.

I continued to telecommute to my job at the same global company; it was a blessing to be able to maintain a salary that could sustain us. Although I was able to meet our monthly expenses, we continued to do without any unnecessary or extra expenses such as cable. While Joe vented less anger toward me and became more collaborative with visitation arrangements, he settled into his routine of not providing any financial assistance. I was torn between forcing him to pay through the court, knowing the anger that would ensue, or simply moving forward with what I had. In the end, I decided it was easier to get by with less. In hindsight, I wish at the time of our divorce I had pushed in our agreement to have the court automatically deduct my support from his paycheck rather than agreeing to manage the effort myself.

I didn't rush to buy furniture for the house either. My once-treasured dining room still sat empty. I hoped that one day it again would be furnished and again become the center for new family traditions and holidays. With that desire still in my heart, sometime after moving back to the house, I received an unexpected phone call from my friend Cherie. "Is your dining room still empty?" she asked.

"Yes," I answered, curious as to why she was asking.

"Well, I've recently been given a dining-room set because one of my grandparents passed away, but my husband and I already have a complete set. Would you be interested in having it?" Before I could respond, Cherie continued, "My husband and his friends are available to move the pieces. You just need to rent a U-Haul truck."

The next weekend, for the price of a truck rental, we were given a full dining-room set, complete with a table, a buffet, and a china hutch. My dining room was once again complete. *How like God*, I thought. He knew how much I wanted a complete dining room. Now for just a fifty-dollar truck rental, I had a beautiful one.

There were other random blessings that dotted our path as well. One such blessing came at the beginning of our first winter back in the house.

"Hey, it's Barb," the voice on the other end of the phone said. It was one of my sisters. "I know this might seem random, but do you have a snow blower?"

"No, why?" I said.

"Our neighbor's buying a new one. They want to give their old one away so they're looking for someone who needs one. They asked if we needed one or if we knew someone who might. I immediately thought of you."

I was thrilled! A snow blower would make surviving the winter far easier and would be safer for me, given my heart issues. On my tight budget, there was absolutely no way I would have been able to afford one. Never would I have dreamt that I could receive one as a gift; that just didn't seem possible! And yet I did.

Another blessing came one spring. I'd had to make some unexpected car repairs, which left my finances tighter than normal. Concerned that my bank account was nearly empty, I asked for prayer over my financial situation at our church's Wednesday prayer service. A week later, as I sorted the mail, I found a plain white envelope between the sales flyers and bills. Curious, as it had no address or postage written on it, I tore the top flap open. Inside was a simple note, "God bless," with money. There was no signature or identifying marks. *Thank You, Lord, for continuing to show me Your promises and love—even through anonymous notes!* I prayed.

Although I had some financial struggles, I realized how blessed I was to have a job that met most of our needs. Having read single-parent statistics, I knew that there was a world of parents struggling to make ends meet. I also understood all too well how hard it was to try to maintain a home on my own. Home projects quite simply didn't always get done because of a lack of time and lack of resources. The more I talked to other single parents, the more I realized unfinished projects seem to come with the territory.

Thankful for what I had, I decided to reach out to the single-adult ministry pastor at my church. Together, we created outreach events that brought teams of volunteers together to help single parents in need. The volunteers selflessly gave of their time to paint and repair homes, clean, and complete tireless hours of yard work. It was wonderful to see their efforts unfold, abundantly blessing the single parents. The first event was such a success that when it was time for the second event, we had more volunteers than we had single-parent homes. With a smile in his voice, the pastor called to let me know that our outreach efforts had one "extra" team of volunteers. Knowing I could benefit from the help, he asked if he could add my name to the list of homes. The next Saturday morning, a team of enthusiastic, wonderful volunteers swooped onto my driveway. The volunteers sanded and painted my porch and garage door, repaired my roof, and completed a tremendous amount of yard work, making my yard sing. What a wonderful blessing! I had set out to focus on others, and the blessing came back to me and my children tenfold. The best part? The enormous testimony it was to my curious neighbors.

But of all the unexpected blessings we received, perhaps the most surprising one came as I watched my children develop a relationship with their dad. His regular visit times provided windows of opportunity for him to engage with them. I realized how hard it was for him. His foundation with them had weakened over the years while au pairs lived with us. Too often, he had been content to let our au pair be the second parent, relieving him of his responsibilities. Then as times became more contentious between us, and the kids picked up on his ill treatment of me, they pulled even further away from him. He had his work cut out for him to establish a new foundation with Jennifer and Ryan. Our children's visits became very valuable to him, causing him to really spend quality time with them.

Quickly, I learned that as a single dad he did many things very differently than I would. I was less than thrilled the first time they came home all smiles sharing that they had cupcakes and bacon for dinner. I desperately wanted to argue with him about his dreadful parenting choices. I also found it hard to watch how he could swoop in for two hours and have nothing but high-energy fun and be able to walk away still full of energy, yet I remained so exhausted. Once visitation progressed to include full weekend visits, I became even more torn. Joe planned wonderful weekends full of activities and fun. Together they ate out at all of our favorite restaurants, and took in local sights—activities not possible on my meager budget. As I struggled to reconcile the joy of watching my children connect with their father, I dealt with resentment that he seemed to have all the fun but none of the responsibility. Struggling, I did the only thing I knew to do: I prayed. *God, what do I do with this? It's so unfair! I'm so exhausted. I have no energy or money. Joe does whatever he wants. He has no responsibility. Please help me deal with this.*

Over time, I was able to let go of the resentment. I knew that if it remained at the center of my attention, it would consume me. God reminded me to instead focus on being the best mom I could be, not on what Joe was or wasn't doing as a father, as long as my children were safe. It took time, but eventually I learned that their occasional very odd dinners of bacon and cupcakes could slide. I knew it wasn't often and if it could help restore a valuable relationship in my children's lives, it was well worth it.

LIFE ON FAST-FORWARD

I've often heard it said that what doesn't kill you makes you stronger. Although I would never wish any of what I have been through on anyone else, I have become the person I am today as a result. I now believe that life is meant to be pursued. We're not meant to sit back and just let it happen. When we are guided by hope rather than fear, we can see that life is full of opportunities waiting to be embraced. It has taken me years to realize that fear drove my decisions for so, so long. I focused so much on the fears of losing a friend, of not being good enough, of being alone. At the time, I didn't realize I wasn't alone in my struggles; everyone struggles with insecurities. But when my focus finally shifted from my fears to God and His power to provide, I was able to face my fears and grow through them even in the darkest times. That is where I finally found true freedom and truly began to live. And that's where you will find freedom too—in shifting your focus to Who, not what. He alone can provide everything you need.

From that June day all those years ago when I fled with an uncertain future until today, I have been amazed at how quickly the time has passed. My children's innocent years of elementary school soon ended. While I treasured the transitions with each step of their growth, I, like any other parent, have felt a twinge of sadness as my children continue to grow, relying on me a bit less with each transition. Together, my family of three continues to lean on God, Who had so tangibly carried us through the toughest years of our lives. Without a doubt, life has taken its fair share of twists and turns.

One unexpected turn came as I navigated life as a single parent. Focused on my children, my faith, and my job, I never set out to meet someone new. Through a work transition, I joined a new team at the same global company that I had worked at for so many years. The new team expanded my network of coworkers to include a great group of people who worked remotely from other parts of the country. Having learned from my previous manager that I needed to find ways to engage with my coworkers, I found ways to let them get to know the real, unguarded me. It didn't take long before one coworker, Jim, and I began confiding in each other. Jim was also a single parent. We shared stories of snowstorms, sledding with our children, and the challenges of parenting solo. Somewhere through the conversations, we realized we both relied on our faith to cope with daily life.

I never expected to meet someone new. But in God's perfect timing, somewhere in my life as a busy mom, I found not just a friend in Jim but a relationship. Despite living several states apart, Jim and I began a friendship that blossomed through long-distance phone calls, e-mails, and eventually weekend visits.

A few years ago Jim and I married; my family of three became a large, blended family. Because of the challenging history I'd had with Joe, it took a lot of prayerful consideration before I could move with my children to another home in another state. Together, Jim and I, along with our kids, established a new home in southern New Hampshire.

Around the same time, Joe and Sarah also married. Looking back at the years of visitation and the unpredictability of Joe, I can see that my children developed a far more stable life in New Hampshire by not visiting with their father as frequently as they had when we lived nearby. His inconsistency in his relationship with them took a greater toll than the distance of the miles. After we moved, we established a schedule of periodic visits, enabling Jennifer and Ryan to spend valuable time together with Joe. He seemed to take their visits less for granted, at least initially, knowing that he wouldn't see them as often. In the end, it fostered a closer relationship than they'd previously had.

My children's elementary school years gave way to middle school, middle school to high school, and then I watched Jennifer and Ryan turn into beautiful young adults. I could fill boastful chapters written by a proud mom about our countless wonderful memories from these precious years. Instead, I'll share just a few.

A few years ago, Ryan proudly played in our town's nationally acclaimed high school band. In addition to their well-attended local appearances, the group travelled to an inaugural parade, the Tournament of Roses, and New York City. Seeing how proud Ryan was to be part of such an esteemed group, I knew how important it was for him to share that with his dad. Putting Ryan's interests higher than my own, I gave an earned free flight voucher to Joe to travel to see one of Ryan's performances. I knew that the opportunity for Ryan to share that accomplishment with his dad was very limited and that it was so important for Joe to see Ryan perform. Joe's visit lasted just two days. But during that time, both Jennifer and Ryan introduced their dad to their friends, a critical part of any teenager's world. And Joe had the proud opportunity to watch Ryan and his band perform at a local stadium.

Last June, together with my parents, my family, Joe, Sarah, and their twin boys, I proudly attended Jennifer's high school graduation. No, there was no group hug at the end of the day, but we came together, putting aside all past differences to honor and support Jennifer as she stepped into a new chapter of young adulthood.

Unlike fairytale endings, life hasn't reached a point where our troubles have simply melted away. Recent years have brought a few interesting challenges. Two years ago my aortic stenosis became severe. The open-heart surgery my doctor told me about all those years ago became a life-saving necessity. The three-hour surgery mushroomed into an eleven-hour ordeal with several weeks of setbacks. My complications didn't end when I began my recovery. During the weeks that followed, my lungs repeatedly filled with fluid. As trying as the recurring issues were, my heart did become stronger with time. Additionally, a complication of scar tissue nearly took my life after it blocked over 90 percent of my left main artery. But these challenges, as so many others in my life, are now a thing of the past. After years of being denied basketball or other activities, I was finally cleared to pursue an active, healthy life.

While changes in life have brought new challenges to our family, these changes also have brought new blessings. Among these blessings are reminders of old blessings—answered prayers from long ago. Shortly after moving to New Hampshire, I found a journal of written prayers from my first years as a single parent. I smiled as I read over my prayer requests, especially my prayers for my children. I was instantly reminded of how faithful God has been in our lives.

One unexpected answer came while my children were in high school. After a corporate restructure, the job that had provided so much flexibility through the transitions of my life was eliminated. That change opened the door to a wonderful opportunity for me to pursue my master's degree. But more important, the corporate restructure led me to a new job opportunity at a local university.

When I found that journal with prayers from all those years ago, I found a page with a prayer for my children. Near the top of my requests, below safety for both Jennifer and Ryan, was a request that somehow college would be affordable to them. I prayed specifically that they could attend with no issue of how they would come up with their tuition payments. I smile when I think of how faithful God is.

On my single-parent income for so many years, I had not been able to save toward their college expenses. Over the years, despite our court order, Joe has not assisted me financially, which made such savings impossible. Rather than facing the challenges that would result if I took Joe to court, I have trusted God. Now Jennifer is a college freshman, attending through a tuition-exchange program between colleges offered by my job. On her heels is Ryan, a high school senior, who is looking forward to attending his first-choice college next fall. Both will be afforded the opportunity to attended college free of tuition payments. Though I am grateful for this tremendous benefit to their future, I have to laugh now because I wish the prayer had also included room and board.

AN UNEXPECTED CALL

Over the years, I have realized that forgiving Joe has allowed me to live the free life I sought for so long. No longer controlled by Joe's manipulative ways, my life has become my own. Still, I've been asked many times how I can even talk to Joe or be in the same room with him. My explanation has never varied: I have genuinely forgiven Joe. Not one ounce of anger remains in my heart toward him. I wish him no ill will, no major tragedy, and I don't even wish what I've gone through upon him. It has been many years since the worst of the drama between Joe and me began.

Last fall, a friend asked me on a whim to attend a women's conference with her. The speaker who touched me the most was Sheila Walsh. She powerfully shared her own story of how God had moved in her life, leading her from brokenness to incredible healing. As I listened to her, gripped by her story, I felt God's whisper that it was time to start writing this book. I couldn't wait to get started. For the first time, I realized that sharing my story could impact others in an incredible way and give them hope in their darkest days.

Then, my story took a new turn. The twist put my emotions and ability to forgive to the test. On a typical weeknight, with our evening routines already well in motion, I found myself in the kitchen making dinner. Jennifer was in our adjacent living room curled up watching TV, nursing a stomach bug. On a commercial break, she decided to return her dad's phone call from earlier in the day. Minutes into the conversation, she began sobbing. I went in to see what was wrong.

"Get Ryan," she mouthed.

Together they talked to their dad for several minutes. When they finished, Ryan handed me the phone.

"Do you have a minute?" Joe asked. His voice trembled, his words audibly swelled with fear and pain. "I'm dying, Susan," he said. "This is going to be what finally gets me. I have terminal cancer."

In that moment, I knew beyond any doubt I had fully forgiven Joe, not only because I could talk to him but because there wasn't a single part of me that found even one ounce of relief or happiness in his pain. In that moment, I stopped doing what I was doing to listen, empathize, and be compassionate.

In the midst of his fear, facing death, Joe revisited a life of bad choices, a life filled with regrets. "You never deserved what I put you through. I am so sorry," he choked out. "Please, if you can ever find it in your heart, please forgive me."

"I forgave you years ago, Joe," I said. "If I hadn't, I wouldn't be talking to you now because I'd still be angry and bitter." I realized those two emotions have always been a litmus test for forgiveness. Too often we say we forgive, yet we hold on to anger for years.

"Joe," I continued, "everything you did is between you and God now. He's the one you need to seek out for real forgiveness."

Joe was convinced that his life of despicable choices now left him without the most important choice yet, the ability to accept forgiveness and salvation offered through Jesus Christ. "I have done too much for God to ever forgive me," he sputtered.

I reminded him of the prodigal son, the son who left home to live a life filled with bad choices only to return home desperate, humbled, and broken. His father welcomed him back with a celebration, not condemnation. Joe too had been a prodigal son, living a life littered with wicked choices. Our conversation perplexed Joe. He struggled to understand why I would care enough to take the time to talk to him.

"It's not about me, Joe," I explained. "If you're dying, you need to get yourself right with God, not with me." I could tell my words swirled around Joe, as though they were a dense fog. He lingered, trying to make sense of a concept that was truly foreign.

After a long pause, he said, "Do you know the things I've done? Do you realize the choices I've made? There's even more than you know." He exhaled before continuing. "Do you remember in court when the judge told you to tell the court where you were living, and my attorney told him we didn't need to know?"

"Yes, I remember," I replied.

Joe sighed again before continuing. "I didn't need to know because I already knew."

Over the course of the next ten minutes or so, Joe detailed how, by the time we reached court, the wheels were already in motion. He had already initiated conversations to have me killed. The only thing that saved me, he explained, was his father, Sam. Joe had shared his plans with Sam after initiating them. Much to Joe's surprise, Sam defended me. "You made her leave," he had explained to Joe. "With the choices you made and the actions you took, she couldn't stay." Sam told Joe that I would always be family to him. He reminded Joe that I was the mother of his children and the mother of Sam's grandchildren. "Not a hair on her head better ever be harmed because of you!" Sam had demanded. In that instant, Sam influenced Joe to stop what he had started. With an additional phone call, the very hit that would have taken my life was cancelled.

Joe sobbed on the other end of the phone as he explained his guilt. Ironically, as he spoke, his pain-filled words made visible the prison he had created for himself. All those years ago, his words and actions had imprisoned me. In the years since, he had been haunted, truly tormented, living in a prison with bars visible only to himself. His guilt and pain limited his ability to ever enjoy life to its fullest.

Tears welled in my eyes as Joe spoke. I was thankful to be safe, alive, and well. I am extremely grateful to Sam, whose influence and words saved my life. More so, I am thankful for God's hand of protection. I should not be surprised to know He was hard at work protecting me from the time I left until today. He promised me that He would keep me safe so that one day I could share this journey. He has been faithful!

Our conversation ended soon after Joe's heavy confession. His voice sounded exhausted from emotions dealing with his own health, but also exhausted from letting go of a burden he had been carrying for thirteen years. I hung up the phone, immediately wanting to comfort the broken hearts of my children.

I spent the rest of the night consoling Jennifer and Ryan. We cried. We hugged. Most of all, we just sat together. My tears were genuine. My heart ached for their overwhelming sadness.

Jennifer choked back tears. "He can't die," she sobbed. "He needs to be at my college graduation. He needs to walk me down the aisle at my wedding." The grief of future memories that might never come to be was truly overwhelming.

Today, more than a year since Joe's original diagnosis, I am happy to report that he is continuing to do well. I pray for his recovery and wish him well.

PURPLE COWS REVISITED

I'm amazed when I reflect upon the remarkable life I have lived, complete with the many fingerprints of a faithful God. Even now, I'm inspired by His remarkable faithfulness as I struggled to survive day to day. I have encountered many inexplicable "coincidences," and when I take time to remember them, they still make me smile. In a world full of people who are dealing with their own battles, I have been blessed by family, friends, and even total strangers who have shared a part, perhaps unknowingly, in my incredible journey. And while I call this "my journey," I believe in reality it is His story; it is a reminder that God still performs miracles, He still answers prayers, and He still very much cares about each one of us. From the time I considered becoming Danielle Matthews, I knew that one day my story would be shared, not so I would be praised or honored, but so that God would receive the glory He deserves for bringing us through.

I find it a bit ironic that it is only now, so many years later, as I sit and write my story that I can finally give new meaning to curious words spoken to my children on a very difficult day in our family history. "Be sure to look for purple cows," the private investigator had said all those years ago.

I admit, I think the kind man who spoke them probably sought only to bring levity to a difficult situation. With compassion, he had hoped to give us something to look forward to, rather than focusing on what we were leaving behind.

On that sunny June day, my children's eyes lit with wonder. "Are there really purple cows where we're are going?" their eyes seemed to ask. Once on the road, with childlike innocence and curiosity, they peered out of my van's windows in wonder as we drove the many miles of our trip. Eventually, with each additional mile behind us, their search for the ever-elusive purple cows faded.

I revisit the search today. I find much profound wisdom in that hopeful, whimsical, seemingly nonsensical phrase. Too often in life we limit ourselves to what can be seen, and we define what is possible by the limits we have experienced. We find ourselves looking for hope in inspirational cards or posters adorned with spectacularly breathtaking photos displaying phrases such as the well-known Bible verse, "With God all things are possible" (Matthew 19:26). Yet, do we believe it? Really believe it? Or do we quickly focus on the words that immediately precede those powerful words: "With man this is impossible"? It is far too easy to discount what lies beyond what we consider possible. We often overlook the presence of God in life, discounting His fingerprints as simply coincidence or happenstance.

Too often, we find it easier to focus on the past, clinging to wounds, words, or other injuries that have gripped us. Sure, we may occasionally look away, then our eyes return to focus on the injury, the hurt, or the anger, but to what benefit? How do we enrich our own lives when our energy is consumed with focusing on the malice that the world has to offer through a lie, a betrayal, an affair, a broken heart, a lost job, or a friend who wronged us? If we allow ourselves to be consumed by those things, if they capture our lingering attention, are we taking the necessary steps to move forward, or are we remaining in a prison made by our own memories and pain? So much in this world fights to gain our attention and our focus. How easy it is to forget that our focus determines our direction. I wonder, what would have been different if Daniel had focused on the lions? We wouldn't consider rewriting his story. How powerful, then, when we use his wisdom to rewrite our own.

The world is full of possibilities far greater than we know. We no longer need to be trapped by our past, by pain, by guilt, or by shame. By choosing to look ahead beyond our own human limitations to focusing on God and His power at work here and now, life can become far more than we could ever imagine.

The world contains far too many people who are unkind, unhappy, or insecure and are ready to tear us down for their own gain. We need not be limited by the opinions of others; they do not define our worth. Nor are we defined by the people in our past, or the people in our present who seek to find how we are different and attempt to use that against us as a weakness. When we refuse to give them that voice of authority in our lives, we can instead hold tight to the value God places in us.

Life can be free of the energy we spend defending our side of a story, our character, or our integrity to individuals who refuse to believe us. Instead, we can seek to live a life that demonstrates who we are, even if others choose not to see our true character. And, we can rest assured that there is nothing that we as individuals ever experience that is not shared by someone else. How freeing it is to know that others have faced our same pain, struggled with similar hurts, and have been broken by the same issues that weigh us down.

In life, we too often hide behind a façade so that those around us think that we have this thing called life all figured out. I certainly did. I know what it's like to want those who encounter us to see us as whole, to think that we've got it all together all of the time. But the reality is that sometimes our life is in pieces. And, if we can't figure out how the pieces fit together, we need only press into God. In His timing, He is faithful and will show us.

I have met many people broken by abuse, rape, infidelity, eating disorders, and a range of other issues. Those hurts seek to become personal prisons, but it doesn't have to be that way. Regardless of the source of our past hurts, we have a loving God Who longs to set us free, if we choose to focus on Him rather than the hungry lions that are eager to devour us. He waits for us to turn our hearts and our eyes to Him.

All those years ago, I was consumed by the pursuit of my own empty dreams. Then I found a sanctuary in the unusual, unlikely place of my car on my commute to work. And that's how God works. It is only when we free ourselves from the noise of life that we can hear Him. He doesn't usually shout into our lives, but is more likely to whisper, stirring our hearts. It is up to us to decide what to do with God's whispers. We need not make ourselves whole on our own. We need not fix ourselves first. When we come broken, hurt, or lost to His feet, He renews us. He *alone* can make us whole.

Over the years, I'll admit, even on my remarkable journey, complete with God's unexplainable presence, it hasn't always been easy to lean on God as faithfully as I did through the most challenging days of my journey. The noise of everyday life has continually tried to crowd out His subtle voice. There have been days when He seemed distant, or perhaps even absent. However, time and time again I am reminded that it is not Him Who has changed but I who have drifted. Then, with conscious effort, my focus returns; encouragement and hope soon follow.

In life, we have a choice: take a chance on what we have not seen and refuse the limits of our own experiences, or continue to live in fear, missing out on all that life has to offer. We can live imprisoned by the opinions of others, or we can refuse their authority to define our self-worth. We can spend our energy defending our side of the story, or instead set out to write our own future. We can remain stuck by insecurities or fear, or we can uncurl our fingers and let go. We can remain angry or find that forgiveness of others sets us free!

Your focus might need just a slight shift in perspective or it may require a complete change in direction. Take time to recognize the presence of miracles all around you. Choose to believe with childlike wonder in what lies ahead, rather than focusing on what you've left behind. Only then can you in earnest begin your own search for purple cows.

RESOURCES

If you or someone you know needs help dealing with domestic violence, reach out to these life-saving resources. These hotlines can connect you with local groups as well as help you create a safety plan for you and your family. Never access online resources on a computer shared with the abuser.

National Domestic Violence Hotline
Annonymous and confidential help available 365 days a year, twenty-four hours a day
(800) 799-SAFE (7233)
(800) 787-3224 (TTY)
thehotline.org.

National Coalition Against Domestic Violence
(303) 839-1852
(303) 839-8459 (TTY)
ncadv.org

SafeHorizon
Crisis counseling in English and Español 24–7.
(800) 621-HOPE (4673)
(866) 604-5350 (TTY)
safehorizon.org
(Link to Español site on home page)

The National Center for Victims of Crime
(202) 467-8700
victimsofcrime.org

Al-Anon Family Groups
Annonymous peer-led meetings and literature for the friends and family members of problem drinkers. English- and Spanish-speaking groups available. Electronic and phone meetings available also.
(888) 4AL-ANON (888-425-2666)
8:00 AM to 6:00 PM EST, Monday – Friday
al-anon.alateen.org (English, Spanish, French)

BIBLIOGRAPHY

Cloud, Henry and John Townsend. *Boundaries: When to Say YES, How to Say NO to Take Control of Your Life*, Grand Rapids: Zondervan, 1992.

Lynch, Chuck. *I Should Forgive, But...2nd Edition: Finding Release from the Bondage of Anger and Bitterness*, Nashville: Thomas Nelson, 1998.

ABOUT THE AUTHOR

Susan Call is a speaker and author who enjoys sharing her insights from life's valleys, offering hope and wisdom to her audiences. She holds a master of science in marriage and family therapy from Eastern Nazarene College and a bachelor of arts in computer science from Susquehanna University. She also studied at Uppsala University and Vilundaskolan in Sweden. Susan lives in New Hampshire with her family. For more information, please visit SusanCall.com.